GOLF ASTROLOGY

Your Pars Are In The Stars!

To Arthur

by

Mark Oman

Keep Swinging!

Mark Oman

Illustrations by Don Jones

Published by Golfaholics Anonymous®
P.O. Box 222357, Carmel, CA 93922
(408) 624-4386 · (408) 626-9357 FAX

Library of Congress Catalog Card Number: 94-096668
ISBN Number: 0-917346-06-8
Printed in U.S.A.

Cover Design by George Foster, Foster & Foster, Fairfield, IA
Interior Design by Liz Turner at Valley Typesetters, Carmel Valley, CA

Special thanks to a great friend and fearless editor, Layne *"The Slasher"* Littlepage.

For my Gemini wife
and "Playing Partner,"
Barbara, Barbara, Barbara,
Barbara...
And all the rest of her
I have yet to meet!

Author's note

No, I am not a world famous astrologer, advisor to movie stars, potentates and President's wives.

I am not a swing guru to the touring pros.

I am a golfer.

For 36 years I have played the game for better, for worse...for richer, for poorer...in sickness and in health, till death do–

You get the idea. I'm just like millions of others whose biggest handicap is loving the game none too wisely, but too well.

Along the way I've discovered some personal truths about the game that have helped me enjoy golf more and play better. These ideas often found their way into many of the books I've written and published.

But nothing to date has made more good common sense than the concepts in *GOLF ASTROLOGY.*

If you don't believe your Astrological Sign has anything to do with who you are and how you perform on the golf course, then read no further and go out and beat balls the way you always have. But just on the chance this "stuff" may have some truth to it, why not take a peek at some of the assets you naturally bring to the game?

What have you got to lose...but your handicap!

TABLE OF CONTENTS

EACH CHAPTER REVEALS

- Your Celestial Golf Symbol

- Your Golf Element

- Your Planetary Golf Guru
  > Identifying the *(Birth Sign)* Golfer
  > Portrait of the Female *(Birth Sign)* Golfer
  > Portrait of the Male *(Birth Sign)* Golfer
  > How *(Birth Sign)* Plays the Mind Game
  > How *(Birth Sign)* Plays the Physical Game
  > Best Part of the *(Birth Sign)* Game
  > Traps 'n Hazards
  > Perfect Foursome
  > Ideal Golf Courses
  > Best Colors to Wear While Playing
  > Shooting Stars for Shooting Pars
  > The *(Birth Sign)* Senior Swinger
  > Your Personal Fairways to the Glory of Golf
  > *(Birth Sign)* Uncensored
  > Famous *(Birth Sign)* Swingers

INTRODUCTION

"Your Birthright to the Glory of Golf"

What kind of golfer are you?
What is your true heart and soul for playing the game?
What are the natural instincts and personality tendencies you bring to golf – the stuff that came as original equipment from your manufacturer – simply, your Birthright as a golfer?

We all come fully equipped with everything we need to succeed at golf. We just don't always know what it is!

For us to get the most out of all the space-age, high-tech, state-of-the-art equipment and instruction out there, we need to get in touch with all the ageless, no-tech, state-of-the-heart stuff inside. We need to connect with our most genuine and natural strengths and weaknesses for the game. Then we can make the most of our strengths and the least of our weaknesses, making our golfing a lot more fun and productive.

GOLF ASTROLOGY was written to help you make that connection to the best and most natural golfer you were born to be. To help you discover the primal instincts and personality tendencies you bring to the game as your Birthright. Simply, the good, the bad, and the beautiful of who you now are as a golfer, and should you desire, how you can change that to enjoy even greater golf in the future.

To do that we will focus primarily on our Sun Sign. While most of us may not know about rising signs, descending signs, planetary positions, or whether we're on or off the cusp, we do usually know our birthday Sun Sign, be it Taurus, Gemini, Libra, etc.

Because our Sun Sign relates strongly to purpose and will, it can give us a great idea of what we need from golf, and what we are willing to do to get it. But our Sun Sign may be even more important because it describes what our hearts really desire – how we truly feel abut our relationship to golf.

The description for each of the twelve Signs in this book should be taken as general information, for we are rarely a pure Libra, Taurus, Virgo, et al. We are far too complex a piece of work for that; as golf is too complex an activity to be defined by any one label we choose to slap on it at the moment.

We must also remember that there's always the inner and outer manifestation of one's basic Sun Sign. A golfer may not look like a particular sign by what he or she says, or how he or she performs, but the forces playing the game inside provide a very different picture. Only YOU know the truth!

This book is really just the first tee – a take off point to the possibilities for inspiration, insight and understanding of why we act the way we do on the golf course.

If this book piques your curiosity to begin a more serious march down these fairways less travelled, then go for it!

If not, let this be an entertaining, safe and fun way to introduce you to just one more kind of handicap-helping enlightenment. This I can promise. Taking a mild, entertaining dose of GOLF ASTROLOGY may not make you the club champion, but it couldn't hurt.

And it could help you become the most natural and best golfer you were born to be.

"Golf is like a grindstone.
Whether it grinds you down or polishes you up,
depends on what you're made of."

ANONYMOUS

It's time to discover what your golf game is really made of.

10

ARIES

March 21 - April 19

GOLFER

Your Celestial Golf Symbol

THE RAM

There is no stopping your charge
through every trap and hazard, every opponent.
Eternally fearless and young at heart,
you just naturally take dead aim and let 'er rip!

Your Golf Element

FIRE

When you get hot, you can burn up the course
with the best of them.
You are an impressive player and others admire your
smoldering passion for the game.

Your Planetary Golf Guru

MARS

With Mars, the God of War, ruling your game plan,
you beat every hole into submission.
You go full bore, firing missiles down the fairway,
knocking down flagsticks with an attacking short game.
You have no qualms about going head-to-head
in a sudden death playoff.
There's nothing you like more
than a good "shootout" with blazing 6-irons!

Identifying the Aries Golfer

Are you the first to tee off at the 19th hole with stories of your own trials and tribulations at the hands of the golfing gods?

Do you have heated one-on-one conversations with your golf ball, clubs, or the forces of nature about their utter lack of cooperation in your battle against the Bogey Beast?

As first sign of the Zodiac, you are the "child" of golf. When you want to play, you don't care what anyone else has planned. You want your golf, now! If you're ready to tee it up, you think the rest of your foursome ought to be ready, anytime, anyplace, anywhere! And you do it with such innocence and enthusiasm that people grab their sticks and join you.

Your love for the game is out there on the course for all to see, with no hidden agenda. Indeed, the Aries golfer possesses the rare courage to call a shank a shank and get on with it!

For you the game is life itself. No matter how golf may beat you down, you always come back for one more round.

"Always throw clubs ahead of you.
That way you don't have to waste energy
going back to pick them up."
TOMMY BOLT

ARIES

Portrait of the Female Aries Golfer

You can survive without golf more easily than any other sign. But when you do get intimately involved with the game, you'll play it your way.

You're not influenced by male golfers and pros who know "the best" way to play. You'll figure that out for yourself.

Golf will not win your heart until you're sure it's worth it. If the game is a pushover, your clubs will be up for grabs at next Saturday's garage sale. Let golf play "hard to get" and you can't resist giving your passion to the chase. For you, getting to be a good golfer isn't half the fun - it's nearly all of it!

Portrait of the Male Aries Golfer

There is nothing secure and laid back about you. You are always hot to trot to tee it up. But when the game disappoints, you can quickly give golf the cold shoulder and walk away.

Anyone who plays golf with you better keep up the pace. You're out there to beat balls, not for a stroll in the park. Friends are sure you invented the line, "The players in the fastest carts always get the best lies."

Your exterior may be calm, but there's a fire in your heart for firing at flagsticks. You are also a club breaker par excellence! And when it comes to club throwing, nobody does it better. (Except perhaps for Taurus.)

How Aries Plays the Mind Game

You are ingenious and love to play the mind game as much as the physical game of golf. You can't wait to try out on the course, or the practice range, the brilliant shots you have played in your head.

You can also be your own worst enemy, becoming intolerant and overly demanding when your golfing desires are delayed.

When you can't beat balls at the range or tee it up for instant gratification, do yourself a favor. Come down off your hot and heavy pursuit of that damnable dimpled little ball. Your handicap will also come down.

How Aries Plays the Physical Game

You are quick thinking, quick moving, and therefore tend to have a faster golf swing. You like to play fast, but have to guard against playing too quick. When the pressure is on, you need to slow down and let your creative powers work their magic.

"Impulsive" describes the way you attack the game. Not only do you make others nervous with your reckless energy, you can short-circuit yourself. Your brain says you need to fade it and your body double-crosses you with a draw or duck hook. Now you're really boiling over!

Slow down and allow some natural harmony and coordination to come back into your swing. Practice a more flowing and connected golf swing with less speed and jerky movement. Do the same with the way you walk the course and waggle at address. As the old Scots say, "As ye waggle, so shall ye swing!"

Best Part of the Aries Game

You're headstrong enough to think you can make any shot, no matter how dangerous, and often do!

If there's the slightest opportunity to make the most of an opponent's or a particular hole's weakness, you will exploit it. The fact that the biggest opportunities usually carry the greatest risk doesn't scare you in the least.

You are fearless - sometimes to a fault.

Traps'n Hazards

You can easily be too aggressive and too competitive for your own good. Playing the safe shot may not suit your heart and soul, but it might help your score.

Your intolerance of slow play, even when unavoidable, makes you hot under your 100% cotton collar. Find an escape valve for the steam coming out of your Ram ears and remind yourself that the game is hard enough without missing a shot before you even hit it!

Perfect Foursome

Leo's bigger than life style makes you feel less outrageous. The mental side of your game is stimulated by Gemini. And, yes, you do have fantasies about lost weekends of hard-core ball-beating with a Scorpio swinger.

Ideal Golf Courses

You like it tough and hot. Palm Springs and Arizona in the summer work for you. Forget tricked up layouts and anything coy or too cute. You want a golf course that says, "Here I am. Want to play me? Take your best shot, but remember, I take no prisoners."

With Mars, the God of War, as your Golf Guru you'd probably enjoy the **Stanley Golf Club** in the Falkland Islands where the rough remains mined from the Argentina-Britain confrontation in the mid-1980's.

The name may sound tame, but **Poppy Hills** in Pebble Beach, California will test your heart and blood pressure. Bring plenty of ammunition and shoot straight or Poppy will waste you.

Perhaps the ultimate test for Aries is the **Koolan Golf Club** in Oahu, Hawaii. Winding in and out about the crater of an ancient volcano, the course measures 7,310 yards from the tips and carries a slope rating of 155, the highest the USGA allows. (It would be 162 otherwise.) Your passion for this hunk of nature in the raw may be tempered by losing as many balls as your handicap index!

Here's a few more courses that ought to keep you fired up:

* **Bayonet Course,** Monterey, California
* **Sheraton El Conquistador,** Tucson, Arizona
* **Eisenhower Golf Course,** *Blue,*
  Air Force Academy, Colorado
* **Cog Hill,** *Dubsdread #4,* Lemont, Illinois
* **The Country Club,** *Open Course,* Brookline, Massachusetts
* **Club Zur Vahr,** *Garlstedter Heide Course,*
  Bremen, Germany
* **Royal Dar-es-Salaam Golf Cub,** *Red Course,* Morocco

Best Colors to Wear While Playing

You see red when your golfing doesn't live up to expectations, so go for it. Gain energy from shirts and pants or skirts in pink, rose, garnet. Wear hot colors that add to your strength as a passionate player for all seasons! Bright warm colors keep you on the birdie trail.

Shooting Stars for Shooting Pars

*   *Because your metal is iron, take full advantage of today's high-tech iron "woods" to ignite a hot round.*

*   *Don't allow your hot exterior to destroy the calm and quiet you need to feel inside to play your best for all 18 holes.*

*   *Be willing to dream the impossible dream, put trust in your gut, and allow good things to happen.*

The Aries Senior Swinger

Of all the signs, you are the youngest at heart. For you golf is the elixir of youth. The older you get, the less the game will be "a war," and more the easy pleasure of pure play. Being a serious adult can be hell on your handicap. Now's the time to lighten up. Be a kid again. For the Aries swinger it's "turn fifty or more, hit the back nine and roar!"

Your Personal Fairways to the Glory of Golf

* *Enjoy the time you have on the course. Not just the ball-striking, but the time in-between.*

* *Learn to appreciate all the game has to offer - particularly when it doesn't deliver the score you ordered.*

* *Without losing your fiery enthusiasm for the game, you'll have more fun and play better when you temper the "hot head" with the cool attitude of a seasoned "been there, done that" player.*

* *Don't let too much passion for the game lead to premature hardening of the handicap.*

* *Balance your personal war with golf with how to play the six-inch course between your ears, and your "Mars will take you to the pars!"*

ARIES

Aries Uncensored

"Lie? I've got no f--ing lie.
I don't even have a f--ing shot!"
MILLER BARBER

"I swear I'm the queen of the lip-out.
The ball comes out and looks at me and grins as if to say,
'Too bad. You missed again.'"
PAT BRADLEY

"The only time I talk on a golf course is to my caddie -
and only then to complain."
SEVE BALLESTEROS

"The only thing I never learned from Billy Martin
was how to knock a guy out in the bar."
JoANNE "Big Mama" CARNER

"Where the ##%%&+@ are the marshals!"
TOMMY BOLT

Seve Ballesteros   JoAnne Carner
Pat Bradley   Joey Sindelar
Meg Mallon   Julius Boros
Dan Pohl   Miller Barber

Ayako Okamoto
Davis Love III
Donna White
Tommy Bolt

Famous Aries Swingers

ARIES

TAURUS

April 20 – May 20

GOLFER

Your Celestial Golf Symbol

THE BULL

You charge after every shot, whether down the fairway
or into the boonies where weaker Birth Signs fear to tread.
You can also be so "bull-headed" that you don't know when to cool your heels
in your relentless pursuit of that red flag waving before your eyes.

Your Golf Element

EARTH

Your connection to golf may be the most solid and practical of all.
You sow the seeds for golfing success with basic good swing mechanics.
Cultivate the more "do-able" aspects of the game by investing time and money in practice,
and then harvest the pars and birdies that bloom in your golfing garden.

Your Planetary Golf Guru

VENUS

Goddess of love! Goddess of your lust for the links!
Venus helps you appreciate the sensuous nature of the game, its lush fairways,
the contours of its bunkers, the mysteries to be discovered in its rough and hazards -
as well as the penalties for playing too fast and loose,
for straying from the straight and narrow!

Venus also helps soften the pain and anguish golf can heap upon your heart
for loving the game none too wisely, but too well.

Identifying the Taurus Golfer

When an irresistible force such as golf meets an immovable object such as Taurus, something's got to give!

You intend to do golf your way. If the game doesn't respond to your mode of attack, you have the patience and persistence to wait it out - until bogeys get bored with you and birdies have had time to feel comfortable in your presence.

But golf can be even more obstinate than you. And one unexpected day it may press you a little too far, tease and torment with one triple bogey too many, and you will paw the ground with your wedge, exhale steam from your nostrils and go "bull-istic!"

Your rage can clear the back nine as you throw the game off your back - along with your bag of clubs, stomping them into broken bits of bad dreams beneath your spiked hoofs.

Once you've dug your spikes into how you're going to beat this game, you're hooked for life.

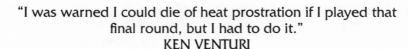

"I was warned I could die of heat prostration if I played that final round, but I had to do it."
KEN VENTURI

TAURUS

Portrait of the Female Taurus Golfer

You have a head for this game and take it seriously. You're not out there to fool around.

Once you make a commitment to play, you stick with golf through good rounds and bad. The game is your friend and real friends don't always act as you would hope - but you still cherish their friendship.

If and when the game returns your loyalty with an endless stream of unplayable lies, bad bounces, and undeserving penalties, golf will be the one to suffer the molten wrath exploding from your Taurus volcano.

When sufficiently provoked, you can go on a rampage, digging deep divots out of the most unfair of fairways, tearing up traps, ripping out rough and happily making a little bonfire of your balls, bag and clubs.

All's fair in love and golf!

Portrait of the Male Taurus Golfer

You're a strong masculine golfer who plays according to the rules of his peaceful Goddess of Love Guru, Venus!

The male Taurus will make his move on golf with a calculating, slow plan of attack, thinking he can sneak up on it, make some great shots and great scores before the game knows it's been won over.

But once golf finds you're on the make to play around, your nature makes you one swinger highly vulnerable to the game's sweet smell of fresh fairways. You are seduced by the tantalizing curvature of a voluptuous par 5 eager to receive every stroke from your biggest drive to your most delicate pitch into scoring position.

If and when you fall for golf, you mean business. You will invest in the necessary equipment, lessons and club membership to show your commitment to a meaningful long-term relationship with the game.

How Taureans Play the Mind Game

You focus on the mechanical aspects of your swing. And once a technique is learned, you hang on to it, even when it no longer works. Your stubborn mind won't let you entertain new ideas that might improve performance. You simply refuse to listen. Eventually you may come around to fresh innovative ideas on how to improve your swing and your course management, but it will be a long slow process before anything new can penetrate your thick hide.

How Taureans Play the Physical Game

You have a body made for golf, and the determination to take the body you have and make it into a golfing form. You do this by beating balls until the cows come home and the mechanics of your swing are branded into every muscle and bone in your body.

Your swing possesses no wasted movement. It is methodical and holds up well under pressure. Every part of your swing has been structured to maximize a high return on investment of energy. But when it goes bad, you are really in trouble because it's hard for you to change and adapt to conditions.

And woe to the foursome behind that tries to rush you. It's not that you actually play slow, you're just eternally... deliberate... in a plodding... ponderous sort of way.

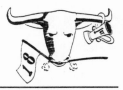

TAVRVS

Best Part of the Taurus Game

Strong, steady and stable -- that's your secret for success as a golfer.

You can outlast most of the terrible shots and painful penalties golf dishes out, which means you can outlast opponents who lack your staying power. It's not necessarily the most exciting way to play or win matches, but you rarely beat yourself. That's for everyone else.

For you, after eighteen holes of grinding competence, patience pays off at the 19th hole.

Traps'n Hazards

You can stagnate and hang on to old thinking and behavior, steadfastly refusing to find a new swing, a new teacher, or a new attitude to help you play better and enjoy golf more.

Lack of adaptability to exciting, fresh, performance-enhancing equipment and techniques may be the most costly trap you continually find your game in. And you seem to make a lot of swings, digging yourself deeper and deeper before you're ready to look up and take a shot in a new direction.

You need to change some of your typical Taurus bull-headedness or give up the chase.

Perfect Foursome

You admire Capricorn's practical approach to golf. You are quite comfortable with Libra's affectionate and deliberate nature. You easily relate to Virgo's love of practice and purity of play.

Ideal Golf Courses

You want a straight-forward, what-you-see-is-what-you-get golf course.

Fairways that wander through a bunch of bumps and blind shots don't qualify for your best course short list. And gimmicky greens that ought to be putted with a bulldozer need not apply.

Being a Taurus, you would feel right at home in Spain, particularly at **Golf Nueva Andalucia** in Marbella. Laid out in a natural bowl beside The Sierra Blanca Mountains, Nueva Andalucia is a big, bad and beautiful course not for the faint of heart. Fellow Taurean, Johnny Miller, holds the course record of 65!

And you must play **Congressional** in Bethesda, Maryland. This is where the last U.S. Open featuring a 36-hole final day was won by Taurean Ken Venturi in 1964. The stamina, patience and sheer guts needed to outlast the terrible heat, humidity, and the greatest golfers in the world is what being a Taurus golfer is all about.

Here are some other play-pens well-suited for Taurus:

* **Olympic Club,** *Lake Course,* San Francisco, California
* **Devil's Paintbrush,** Caledon Village, Ontario
* **Prairie Dunes,** Hutchinson, Kansas
* **Firestone,** *South Course,* Akron, Ohio
* **Oakmont,** Oakmont, Pennsylvania
* **Southern Hills,** Tulsa, Oklahoma
* **Grand Cypress,** *The New Course,* Orlando, Florida
* **Pebble Beach,** California

(Play a modern Pete Dye design such as **PGA West,** *Stadium Course* in Palm Springs and a true Taurus may not only lose his balls, but also both ears and a tail!)

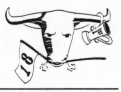

TAURUS

Best Colors to Wear While Playing

As you would expect from such a rock-solid, down-to-earth sign, you play your most steady game when adorned in golden brown, copper brown, reddish brown, and ultra brown.

But it wouldn't hurt your game and wardrobe to lighten up. A wild beige-on-beige ensemble will not make anyone think you're auditioning for your club's Halloween party.

Shooting Stars for Shooting Pars

* *You don't always use your creative flair for the game. It's there, just below your top-soil. Dig down and let fly those creative "Bogey-Busters" buried inside.*

* *Believe in yourself. Just because the rest of your foursome ignores your advice, doesn't mean you shouldn't take it.*

* *Lighten your thinking to get your handicap sinking!*

The Taurus Senior Swinger

Now's the time to let go of your old game plan and open up to all you can achieve as a senior player.

You may not have reached the level of play you have worked long and hard for, but the game has given you a Mulligan.

Golf can be lovelier the second time around. Relax. Allow yourself the freedom to do what seemed impossible for you in younger years - experiment!

Play golf for the simple joy of playing the game. You will be rewarded beyond your wildest bull-headed dreams.

Your Personal Fairways to the Glory of Golf

* *Your challenge as an earth-bound Taurus golfer is to look down at fairways rather than keeping your mind six feet under looking up at the roots.*

* *Release your spirit of adventure. Trade your Taurean horns for some mouse ears and go play a wild cartoon golf course - just for the fun of it!*

* *With your practical, conservative approach to the game, you rarely give in to your more passionate longings for experimentation. Go ahead. Let the shaft out and swing from the heels. It will do your heart and soul good.*

* *Do not be so stuck in the mud of middle-of-the-fairway thinking that you lose out on the thrills and surprises only found on golf's fairways less travelled.*

* *You can grind so hard that you grind all the best stuff out of golf - like fun and enjoyment.*

* *Dare to be a bull of a different brand. Use your imagination. Imagination is the voice of daring!!*

TAURUS

Taurus Uncensored

"Everyday I try to tell myself this is going to be fun today.
I try to put myself in a great frame of mind before I go out -
then I screw it up with the first shot."
JOHNNY MILLER

"After you get the basic abilities down,
it's all mental."
KEN VENTURI

"As long as your number - two power accumulator doesn't
break down, you can reach maximum centripetal force with
minimum pivotal resistance."
MAC O'GRADY

"I can't win anything but money."
FRANK BEARD

"Gentlemen, play golf.
And if you aren't a gentleman when you start,
after the crushing events of the game, you surely become one."
BING CROSBY

Ken Venturi
Bing Crosby
Betty Jameson
Hal Sutton

Johnny Miller
LiselotteNeumann
Harry Vardon
Tim Simpson

Betsy Rawls
John Mahaffey
Mac O'Grady
Frank Beard

John Daly
Dale Eggeling
Leo Diegel
Wm. Shakespeare*

Famous Taurus Swingers

*Who really said, "To golf or not to golf, that is the question?"
Only Taurus knows the answer.

TAURUS

GEMINI

May 21 – June 20

GOLFER

Your Celestial Golf Symbol

THE TWINS

Depending on which of you shows up on the first tee,
you can play like Tom Watson or Dr. Watson, swing like Amy Alcott or
Louisa May Alcott, drive it dead solid perfect like Greg Norman or
Stormin' Norman Schwartzkoff!
(Actually, they both hit it pretty good.).

Your Golf Element

AIR

The social aspect of golf appeals to you.
It is the nature of your air element to form relationships with those you golf with.
You probably won't find the great love of your life here -
unless it's golf - but you will find good friends and playmates.

Your Planetary Golf Guru

MERCURY

Not all of us are fortunate enough to have the Winged Messenger of the Golfing Gods
as our personal Guru specializing in commerce and communication.
You know exactly what to say to get the most strokes on the first tee
in order to collect the most money on the last green!

Why are you so good at improvising a new shot on the spot?
You can thank your Winged Mercury for your quick thinking.
Fastest of the planets, Mercury keeps you playing the game at a good clip.
Slow play? No way! Not with Mercury as your partner.

Identifying the Gemini Golfer

Is the front nine agony and the back nine ecstasy? Brilliant course management on the toughest holes and loosy-goosy mistakes on the easiest? The smartest player one day, and the next, dumbing your way around eighteen holes?

Your golf embodies all the good, the bad, the beautiful and the ugly of the game from one round to the next - even from one shot to the next!

Gemini is ever on the move. He or she usually talks fast, listens faster, and swings even faster.

Then again, a Gemini might exhibit the very opposite tendencies, depending on which one of you shows up. For you are not so much twins as multiple personalities. Most of them are charming to play with and will tell you more than you ever wanted to know about your golf game - and theirs.

Gemini and golf? Definitely a roller coaster ride on the Golf Agony and Ecstasy Express.

Gemini can say, "That's it! I quit! Never again!" And seconds later when offered a tee time at a great new course, Gemini adds, "Well... as long as I'm going to quit, I might as well get in one last round."

"Golf got complicated when I had to wear shoes and begin thinking about what I was doing."
SAM SNEAD

GEMINI

Portrait of the Female Gemini Golfer

Your golfing friends are always curious - and nervous - as to which one of you will show up to play. If it's a social game, they can relax. Most of your other selves are scratch players when it comes to the gift of gab. But if it's a tournament, your fellow players may pray that several of your other selves are out of town for the day.

You can be passionate about the game, practice regularly and be a strong partner or a formidable opponent. Then at the Club Invitational the following week, for no apparent reason, you ride around the course on your broomstick stirring up a fine double-bogey brew of humiliation and heartbreak.

Whatever is bothering you gets thrown into Pandora's golf bag all week long. When you get to the course, it all comes out. Tee off on number one, and you're teed off for the next four or five hours!

Wouldn't it be great if you could only stop thinking for a while and just play? But then you wouldn't be a Gemini.

Portrait of the Male Gemini Golfer

"Have clubs, will travel" is your motto. You need to keep moving, and are always ready to play a new course whenever you've got the chance and wherever it is.

You like to play with a lot of people. The more, the merrier. As Willie Nelson said, "No more than twelve to a foursome!"

If you can't get anyone to join you, that's okay too. Even playing alone, you've got a great foursome.

Your fickle attitude about golf drives friends crazy. One day you're dead serious about taking lessons and beating balls. Then, after one really ugly shot, you plan to devote your remaining years to skydiving or becoming a bullfighter. Then the other side of you figures out how to correct that ugly shot and talks you back into the game - for the 96th time this year.

How Gemini Plays the Mind Game

You can be brilliant, creative and analytical, a winning combination. Golf allows you to use all the mental powers you possess. But you are never satisfied with your game because you seek perfection in a pursuit that can never be completely mastered. Golf will be forever frustrating and disappointing. When the game no longer engages your active mind or doesn't live up to expectations, you can sulk like a champion.

How Gemini Plays the Physical Game

You are agile and have great hand and foot work!

You have to keep moving and your golf swing does just that. A one-piece continuous swing with great tempo and rhythm fits you perfectly. But with Gemini's nervous energy, you have to watch out for swinging too fast.

Fortunately, your Mercury Guru generates more energy to the brain than your body, or your swing would be even faster.

Slow down. Practice a longer, flowing swing and get some sleep before an important match. When your ever-active mind keeps you awake, the body energy isn't there when you need it.

Gemini has the grace of a dancer, so find a song with a tempo you like. Play it in your head and swing to it on the course. You may find "gettin' to the dance floor" was never easier.

GEMINI

Best Part of the Gemini Game

You are able to react quickly and creatively to whatever situation you find yourself in. Your "other selves" have the ability to see several ways of playing any shot, no matter how impossible it might seem from one point of view.

The best part of your game is that it comes into play when you're in trouble and need it the most! Where so many other signs are weak at improvising, you have no trouble changing according to the conditions at hand.

Geminis have the great ability to dance to whatever music golf is playing.

Traps'n Hazards

You have so much nervous mental energy that it's hard for you to relax when you're in a tight match - even when it's only against your other selves!

Tight muscles hurt your short game the most when you need a feel for chipping and putting. And when your short game goes, so can your temper. And, yes, you are harder on yourself than other signs are, probably because there are so many of you to blame.

But perhaps your biggest trap is always wanting to try something new. Your active mind and extravagant nature make you a glutton for every new piece of high-tech, space age, state-of-the-art equipment to come out.

Perfect Foursome

Next to three of your other selves, you genuinely like the flamboyance of Leo. Libra provides a much needed calming influence, whether you admit it or not. But you and Aquarius can really ham 'n egg it in a best-ball format when you both get into the music golf's playing that day.

Ideal Golf Courses

Your social nature will fit right in at Sam Snead's old playground, **The Greenbrier,** White Sulphur Springs, West Virginia. And your many personalities will all have a chance to shoot their best shots when playing at **Pinehurst's** many great courses - particularly #2, #6, #7, **Pine Needles** and **Mid Pines**.

With Mercury as your Guru, you'll have no trouble keeping the pace at the **Brickyard Crossing** where four holes are inside the Indy 500 Speedway.

To feel like you're in Scotland, you only have to travel to the Monterey Peninsula for **Spanish Bay**, the closest thing America has to a true seaside Scottish links course. Here you'll get a chance to try every club in the bag, and every shot your many selves can come up with. You'll need 'em all!

When you're ready for a big-time Gemini getaway, you may want to try the following itinerary:

*   Monday on **Merion,** *East,* in Pennsylvania...

*   Travel to tee it up on Tuesday at **Tuernberry,** Scotland...

*   Wednesday, you walk the wild side of **San Lorenzo Golf Club** in Portugal then...

*   Thursday, and you're on a golf safari across the **Karen Country Club** in Nairobi...

*   Friday, you fly to the fabulous fairways of **Wack Wack Golf Club** in Manila...

*   Saturday, it's off to the **Phoenix Resort & Country Club** in Kyusha, Japan, a little sake and sayonara...

*   Sunday, it's the Big Island of Hawaii with the **Mauna Kea** in the morning and Mahi Mahi and the moon at night...

*   And finally back to Monday and **Vallescondido** in Mexico City and a long, long siesta.

GEMINI

Best Colors to Wear While Playing

You look hot in the cool tones of navy blue, aqua or gray. But you can also be hot in the warmth of yellow.

Depending on which of your personalities is playing, stick with one or the other color. Then again, today's round may require the services of several of your in-house support team, in which case you may want to wear a rainbow. After all, you're a Gemini!

Shooting Stars for Shooting Pars

* *You can be very open to good ideas from better players. Now all you have to do is listen to them!*

* *Because it's easier for you to get your thinking in the groove than your swing, spend a little more time on the range with your swing and give your head trip a rest.*

* *Want to play better? Think about the communication that starts from your heart, not just your head.*

The Gemini Senior Swinger

You are the Peter Pan of golf. With all your personalities, you have the ability to remain youthful in body and mind seemingly forever!

To enjoy golf more as you grow older, get off the perfection merry-go-round, which hasn't always been so merry. Remember, "Bees aren't as busy as you think. They just can't buzz any slower." But you can!

Now's the time to turn the brain "buzz" down a few notches and find a comfortable balance between all your selves.

Play the world's golf courses just for the fun of it. It's play time!

Your Personal Fairways to the Glory of Golf

* *You brilliantly share your ideas about the more esoteric whys and wherefores of golf. When you become just as brilliant a listener, you will begin to transcend your handicap.*

* *Changing courses, equipment and your swing is easy. Changing the way your personalities play against each other is your challenge. Now's the time for finding harmony, so you can dance with all those Bogey Beasts within, rather than trip over them.*

* *You have a lot of casual friends in golf. Relax and get out of your mental gymnastics, and you may find even stronger relationships that nurture your heart and soul.*

* *Stay in the present. Today's round, this shot, is all you've got. Feel it. Play with it. Enjoy it. Too late to replace yesterday's divots. Can't miss tomorrow's putts until you stroke 'em. Today is all you have.*

GEMINI

Gemini
Uncensored

"Golf is the hardest sport... One day you're up on cloud nine
and the next day you couldn't scratch a whale's belly."
SAM SNEAD

"I was a complete bleep-bleep for three or four years there.
My game didn't improve until I stopped doing
all that nonsense. I'm still an emotional player,
but I have it under control... I hope."
CRAIG STADLER

"Some players would complain if they were playing
on Dolly Parton's bedspread."
JIMMY DEMARET

"If you watch a game, it's fun. If you play it, it's recreation. If
you work at it, it's golf."
BOB HOPE

"My goal is to become filthy rich.
But obviously, that isn't going to be in golf.
I'm working on a stock market fraud."
GARY McCORD

Bob Hope
Laura Baugh
Jimmy Demaret
David Graham

Hale Irwin   Phil Michelson
Glenna Collett Vare   Shelley Hamlin
Gary McCord   Mark Calcavecchia
Craig Stadler   Sandra Haynie

Sam Snead
D.A. Weibring
Gary Hallberg
Marilyn Monroe

Famous Gemini Swingers

GEMINI

CANCER

CANCER

June 21 – July 22

GOLFER

Your Celestial Golf Symbol

CRAB

Your extremely sensitive, emotional nature means that when you're not playing well or the game plays one of it's nasty little jokes on you, you'll crawl inside your hard shell and sulk. Or you'll just be really crabby about the game.

Your Golf Element

WATER

You are the first of the water signs and your golfing energy and emotions are directed inward to the darker depths of your being. As a water sign, you understand how to go with the flow of the game rather than fight the tide.

*For you, golf has to be a comfortable place to come home to.
The golf course is your home away from home - a safe haven from the outside world.*

Your Planetary Golf Guru

MOON

The moon shines upon your golf game, filling you with compassion for those less fortunate golfers who have yet to find the emotional nourishment the game can offer. Understanding how golf plays upon your feelings can help you become a stronger player - and better able to help others achieve a healthier balance for the game.

Let your Moon Guru light the way to transform your negative emotions into powerful positive action.

Identifying the Cancer Golfer

Do you like to play night golf with moonlit fairways and glow-in-the-dark balls?

No, you're not a vampire. But if you like to play in the moonlight and shadows on a warm summer night, you are a Cancerian golfer.

The moon in its many forms is the key to your golf game. Its moods flow high and wild, then low and lonely like the ocean's tide.

You are not particularly passionate about golf, but when it's good, you bask in the glow of your own golfing grandeur. When the tide goes out, taking the best parts of your golf game with it, the moon is blue and so are you.

One of the things you seek from any pursuit is material security. You get that in golf by hanging on to "stuff." You probably have a closet or garage full of old clubs, bags, shoes, practice nets, a zillion hats and old shag balls. Unfortunately, you also hoard old thinking and negative emotions. Constant worry about your game can lead to collecting some golf ball-sized stuff in your gut.

Your trips to the "pars" by the light of your silvery moon can lead dangerously near the edge of a well of deep pessimism about ever playing happily again.

And while there is much you hide in your hard shell personal fortress, your face tells the tale of your suffering and your ecstasy. Golf is indeed an x-ray into your soul. What you are on the golf course speaks so loudly it doesn't matter what you say when explaining it at the 19th hole!

"It's tough for me to play any tournament.
There's no week of the year I wouldn't rather be home."
BRUCE LIETZKE

CANCER

Portrait of the Female Cancerian Golfer

As a true moon child, the sound of the ocean fills you with great creative energy. You enjoy playing golf accompanied by the soothing sound of the surf.

The way you play is very connected to the ocean in that your ball-striking and overall enjoyment of the game come over you in waves. When your "surf" is up, it can be a wild ride for a few holes. Just as quickly you can flatten out and quietly sink into a dark canyon just offshore.

Golf would be more fun if you could always play in the light of the moon. That will always be your best starting time.

And you don't always have to play the safest shot. Take a chance. The worst that can happen is losing a ball or two. It won't break your bank account. How are you going to find more balls if you don't have a good reason to be tramping around in the rough?

And don't worry. You will never spend too much on golf. You may be feeling low and decide a new set of high-tech clubs will awaken some dreams, but you won't rob your piggy bank to pay the pro. At least not until he or she agrees to let you hold a Midnight Madness Tournament during the next full moon!

Portrait of the Male Cancerian Golfer

You are not the easiest golf partner to get to know.

Your moods move across the golf course as fleetingly as sunlight and shadows - about as fast as you can go from laughter to crankiness.

You don't feel obligated to go public with that pain. You'd rather crawl into your private shell and let your silence do the talking, a big asset if the guy you're trying to beat is also sharing the golf cart with you. But no matter what you put your golfing partners through, you are sensitive to their feelings and a very loyal friend.

How Cancer Plays the Mind Game

You are quick to respond to all the surrounding conditions of play. You note the placement of pin locations on passing holes yet to be played. You're aware of the speed of the greens. You have a feel for the wind and are good at judging a one- or two-club breeze. And you collect and store everything you need to know about the golfers you're playing with - particularly if one of them is your opponent.

On the down side, you can dredge up past poor performances and wallow in their cold muddy waters. Worse, you are all too receptive to other players' negative outpourings.

Just because you have enormous sympathy for other golfers' pain doesn't mean you have to live it for them!

How Cancer Plays the Physical Game

Methodical, deliberate and very protective is how you approach the physical part of golf. You are side-movement oriented and need to stay centered during your swing and rotate your body, rather than sway from side to side.

Golf is in good hands with Cancer. Your hands can. and should be the most important element of your swing. Use them to your advantage.

Don't be indecisive during your swing. Make your decisions before you step up to the shot, then put it on automatic pilot and take a healthy whack at the ball.

CANCER

Best Part of the Cancerian Game

You have a natural talent for storing all the information necessary to play well. You are aware of the course environment, conditions of play and temperament of your partners and opponents.

And you use that information creatively. You can also be very patient with your game and will persevere when others are ready to give up.

Traps'n Hazards

You've got the first club you ever bought or were given as a child. Just looking at your first putter gives you a warm feeling. But living in the past can rob you of a more productive and satisfying present.

When you listen to your powerful positive inner voice, you'll be less inclined to rely on old thinking when confronted with the unknown.

Perfect Foursome

Capricorn company gives you a good secure feeling, and you need all you can get. You definitely enjoy the easy communication of Gemini. And Pisces can always be counted on to lift you out of your blue lagoon water hazards.

Ideal Golf Courses

You are the home lover of the Zodiac and your home course is your castle. For you, familiarity doesn't breed contempt, it breeds birdies!

While others may sample the fairways and greens of shapely, exotic courses far and away, you would just as soon swing in the comfort of your own backyard. Like the theme song from "Cheers," you want to play where everyone knows your name.

When you do travel, you'll feel right at home at **The Homestead** in Hot Springs, Virginia. It's been there forever. It's comfortable, and each of its three courses has its own club house and professional.

The Carmel Valley in California has two great resorts for the Cancer golfer to snuggle into. **The Golf Club at Quail Lodge** winds in and about the Carmel River and has all the creature comforts and quiet luxury to soften the hardest Cancer shell.

A short pitch and putt up the river is the **Carmel Valley Ranch**, whose amenities and redesigned course may be the most "golfer friendly" Pete Dye design anywhere.

You may feel a certain instinctive connection to the **Pit Golf Links** in Pinehurst, North Carolina, since the course was carved out of an old sand quarry. The fact that sand and water come into play on nearly every hole should help Cancer play in virtual primordial bliss.

Some other comfy courses for Cancer include:

* **Black Butte Ranch**, Sisters, Oregon
* **Hills of Lakeway,** Austin, Texas
* **Ojai Valley Inn & Country Club,** Ojai, California
* **Port Ludlow Resort,** Port Ludlow, Washington
* **Magnolia, Palm, Lake Buena Vista, Eagle Pines, and Osprey Ridge,** Disney World, Orlando, Florida
* **All 80 courses in Myrtle Beach,** South Carolina

CANCER

Best Colors to Wear While Playing

If you can't play by the light of the silvery moon, wear it! Silver, opalescent watery hues, pale green and smoky colors help you play your most enlightened golf.

Shooting Stars for Shooting Pars

* *Have more confidence in your intuitive powers to make the best decisions on the golf course. Intuition may be the strongest club in your bag.*
* *When your mood swings become less intense and more controllable, so will your golf swings and score.*
* *There's a time for moody blues in the moonlight and time to let the sunshine in. When you get to the course, get out of the car, crawl out of your shell, and soak up some rays. It'll be healthy for your handicap.*

The Gemini Senior Swinger

As you get older, your home course becomes even more of a safe haven protected by a moat, where you can play surrounded by comfortable old friends and familiar fairways.

By now you should have enough inner security not to fear what the future holds. Try some new, high-tech oversize clubs. You can always go back to that old rusted set stashed safely in the closet. Or give those old clubs to a youngster you're helping to learn the game.

Your Personal Fairways to the Glory of Golf

* *Your Moon Guru lights the way to golf's warm hearth. All you have to do is follow the fairway and put trust in those intuitive flashes of understanding and clarity.*

* *Refuse to be bogged down in quicksand traps of old behavior. Any golfer can remember the past. Players with real imagination remember the future!*

* *A new hot ball, hot putter, driver or complete set of new clubs might be just what your Golf Guru ordered. Loosening your pocketbook outside could loosen some peak performance attitudes inside.*

* *Give yourself a break. Isn't the game hard enough without being a surrogate sufferer for your friends' golfing misfortunes?*

* *The song "Blue Moon" has always been a broken record in your golf game. It's time to hit it O.B. and start swinging to a new theme, "The best is yet to come!"*

CANCER

Cancer
Uncensored

"That little white ball won't move until you hit it
and there's nothing you can do after it has gone."
BABE DIDRIKSON ZAHARIAS

"I never really dreamed of making many putts.
Maybe that's why I haven't made many."
CALVIN PEETE

"When I get serious - or bitchy - I don't play well."
LAURI MERTEN

"Try chipping to a tape of either REO Speedwagon
or a Huey Lewis and the News.
It does wonders for your game."
JULI INKSTER

"Children soften you up a lot.
You come back home, toys everywhere, think 'ok'
and get down on your knees and play.
And you forget about golf."
NICK FALDO

Bruce Leitzke
Lauri Merten
Mike Reid
Lee Elder

Babe Zaharias
Billy Casper
Robert Gamez
Gene Littler

Julie Inkster
Calvin Peete
Stephanie Farwig
Roger Maltbie

Nick Faldo
Charles Coody
Colin Montgomerie
Old Tom Morris

Famous Cancer Swingers

CANCER

LEO

July - August 22

GOLFER

Your Celestial Golf Symbol

LION

When a foursome of Leo golfers tee it up, it's definitely a pride of Lions.
You can't help it if your powerful personality and larger-than-life
love for the links puts you above the crowd.
Your Lion heart is full of enthusiasm for all the game has to offer.
And you have the courage and charisma to lead less endowed players
to golf's promised fairways.

Your Golf Element

FIRE

Not only do you have the heart of a Lion,
but also the burning desire to show friends and the world how you can beat
the golf course by the sheer power of your personality.
But be careful. The intensity of your internal fire for golf
can also become your biggest handicap.

Your Planetary Golf Guru

SUN

How can you be anything but a forceful and radiant player
when your Golf Guru represents the cosmic life force?
While you need to feel that you shine as bright as the sun,
your fame will glow longer if you turn down the fire.
Don't let your golf intensity lead to premature burnout.

Identifying the Leo Golfer

You were born to rule the golfing roost. The Big Cat on the course, you're not shy about letting everyone know it.

For you, a round of golf is like going on safari, and you are the "King of the Golf Jungle."

Armed with nothing but the best weapons, you stalk the course in search of birdies and big game eagles while keeping that ever-lurking Bogey Beast at bay.

You take great pride in your golf accomplishments. Your enormous ego, which needs all the strokes it can get, is overshadowed only by your giant Lions heart for the game. Because you play from the heart, you must feel good about your game, and yourself, to play your best.

You love the challenge, the game, and your fellow big game shooters, but you call the shots; and your swing, your putter, and your ball must obey!

Once everyone - opponents and your golf ball - knows who's in charge here, you can be surprisingly bright and playful even to the point of stretching out in the sun for a lazy snooze when the hunt slows on the back side safari.

When you have the scent of your "par" prey, you stick to your path. No matter what trouble you may encounter along the trail, it's difficult for you to change course. You often slink right into the trap of your greatest enemy, the Bogey Beast.

If someone else could practice the boring two-foot putts leaving you to practice the bigger shots, you would make them feel so honored that they would pay you for the privilege. They'd also be afraid you'd bite off their head if their practice didn't improve *your* game!

"I'm glad to have brought this monster to its knees."
BEN HOGAN
(After winning the 1951 U.S. Open)

LEO

Portrait of the Female Leo Golfer

You light up the course and the lives of those you play with. The leader of your pack, you conduct tournaments and social club business the way it should be done.

You have little trouble convincing everyone that your way is the right one. Your genuine warmth and radiant smile conquer all. If that's not enough equipment to succeed in the world of golf, you've got a bagful of beauty, charm, vivacity, sensuality, charisma and ambition to use on the game - and anyone who would usurp your rightful place in control of your ladies-in-waiting.

Let anyone attempt to remove you from your throne, and they will find that it's not your putting that's gotten sharper, but your claws inside those golf gloves.

People excuse your occasional strolls down those private fairways of vanity and arrogance because you are genuinely kind, compassionate and extremely generous.

Portrait of the Male Leo Golfer

If anyone is made for the spotlight and pressure of a big tournament, it's you. You must have an audience in order to light up the course.

Doesn't sound like you? You're just a gentle pussy cat who purrs down the fairway?

It's an act. Given the slightest opportunity to blind the opposition with your golfing brilliance, you raise your proud head and take a big bite out of a difficult hole or dangerous shot.

You have a ferocious appetite for the game, and sometimes you bite off more than you can chew.

If your favorite clubs don't live up to their promise, or a course no longer responds to your "advances," you can become a roaring club-breaking beast.

If and when golf fails to fill your giant heart, you may crawl away and lick your wounds for a long, long time.

How Leo Plays the Mind Game

You have it all nailed down in your head. The set-up, stance, grip, waggle, is all fixed in a strong routine.

You've got the mind game figured out and you're prepared to show it off in action - if only to prove to your fellow golfers you can make it work.

Your decisiveness is very good for golf, but once you've made up your mind how to play a round, a hole, or a particular shot, you go full bore - even when new conditions require a new plan of attack.

Sand, water, trees, wind and rain better stay out of your way when you're on the prowl for birdies. You are not about to let them play through!

Playing mind games to defeat your opponent is beneath your dignity. If the strength of your magnetic personality, the powerful energy, fighting spirit and strong heart of Leo is not enough to win the day, you will not stoop to such low-life deceit as mind-messing. You are bigger than that.

How Leo Plays the Physical Game

You stalk each hole, head forward, ready to pounce on a bird with your whole body. Your arms and hands are very important in your swing, but can hurt you when they get too fast, hard, and aggressive through impact.

For you to make the most of your swing, you need to focus on a relaxed and softer grip, then move those arms through the ball in a more gentle, flowing fashion. With a less forward-leaning stance and a better balance point a little back from your toes, you'll be able to release all that Leo energy through the ball.

LEO

Best Part of the Leo Game

The more important the game, the better you play! You rise to the occasion with courage and dignity.

You respond to an important match with a full heart and a steeltrap mind. And you are disciplined enough in your ambitions for golfing glory that when the game gets tough, you get tougher.

Not only can you stand the heat of a big match, you live to perform on that hot spot.

Traps'n Hazards

You can set impossibly high standards of play and feel miserable when you don't live up to them. This can lead you to be lazy, an over-reaction to all the burning desires and intensity that went before.

Your self-containment can hide a lot of emotional stress. You have a tendency to argue with the only truly worthy opponent you face on the golf course - yourself.

Will Rogers meant you when he said, "Golf can make you so mad at yourself, you forget to hate your enemies!"

Perfect Foursome

Sagittarius makes the game an adventure. You play well with Libra, a good social and peaceful partner. And you enjoy the golfing good times so much with Pisces that you could play around with them forever.

Ideal Golf Courses

You prefer to play on the great golf stages of the world. Playing no-name, low profile courses would be like asking a great actor to play off-off-off-Broadway!

You need to play at the best clubs and enjoy the most lavish facilities for lunch, dinner, massage… the little things that make a commitment to golf worthwhile. Poorly maintained or esthetically unpleasant surroundings don't inspire you. The course must sparkle and shine brightly or there's no glow for you to bask in.

The British commentator, Henry Longhurst, said it all for Leo: "Golf is the only game where one can perform on the great battlegrounds where the mighty have made history."

For you to play your best, you need to prowl the fairways where the kings and queens of golf have reigned:

* ***Royal Troon***	* ***Royal Birkdale***
* ***Royal Melbourne***	* ***Royal Montreal***
* ***Royal Adelaide***	* ***Royal St. George's***
* ***Royal Swaziland***	* ***Royal Lytham & St.Anne's***
* ***Royal Dornich***	* ***Royal Portrush***
* ***Royal Selangor***	

* ***Royal Koninklijke*** in Belgium (Where if you can pronounce it, they'll let you play it!)

If these are not in your neighborhood, you may have to settle for:

* ***Merion Golf Course,*** *East,* Ardmore, Pennsylvania
* ***Seminole,*** North Palm Beach, Florida
* ***Los Angeles Country Club,*** *North,* Los Angeles, California
* ***Cypress Point,*** Pebble Beach, California
* ***Colonial,*** Fort Worth, Texas

LEO

Best Colors to Wear While Playing

One of the most fashionable Leo golfers of all time, Doug Sanders, hit it pure when he said, "Never wear hand-me-downs, freebies, borrowed togs, or Christmas presents."

With the sun such a part of your life force, you will be an even more powerful golf force when wearing the high energy hues of gold and yellow and the hot orange glow of the setting sun.

Shooting Stars for Shooting Pars

* *What you are on the golf course roars so loudly, it doesn't matter what you growl later when you try to explain it.*
* *Better balance between all parts of your game - inside and out - will bring you more admiration from other golfers than anything you can say.*
* *You don't have to dominate golf to get better. Play with it and golf may take more kindly to playing with you!*

The Leo Senior Swinger

Here's your chance to mellow out. You don't have to be the best golfer at your club, or even in your foursome. Being second to someone else doesn't mean you're not first with those family and friends most important to you.

You'll never lose your youthful enthusiasm for the game, so now is the time to share your love of golf with those who need your shining smile and positive outlook.

The older the Leo, the bigger the heart from which to give away the lessons of golf's life force.

Your Personal Fairways to the Glory of Golf

* *Go ahead, let someone else take center "fairway." Remember, a supporting role can often be more fun and memorable than the star part.*

* *When you reduce the heat of your intensity and soften your roar, you'll focus less on your fear of failure and more on the challenge, excitement and fun of the hunt.*

* *Because you view your performance on the course like that of an actor on stage, you must not let your need for satisfying the rest of your foursome, or a gallery, wear out your Leo heart.*

* *You can be all you are without having to prove it. When you believe in the natural attributes you bring to the game, you won't need to seek acclaim from others.*

* *One of the great Leo swingers, Mae West said, "Too much of a good thing is wonderful." But it can also be too much! When it comes to golf, "the harder you try, the more strokes go bye-bye."*

LEO

Leo
Uncensored

"I play with friends. But we don't play friendly game."
BEN HOGAN

"This course sucks!"
KEN GREEN

"I've been known to party day and night.
In Las Vegas, I paid a guy $50 an hour to sleep for me."
DOUG SANDERS

"I never swore in my whole life til I met her."
DOUG MOCHRIE
(husband & caddie)

"That's a damn lie!"
DOTTIE MOCHRIE

"I'm only scared of three things –
lightning, a side-hill putt, and Ben Hogan. "
SAM SNEAD
(Gemini)

Ben Hogan
Bobby Wadkins
Janet Coles
Ken Green

Dottie Mochrie
Wayne Grady
Doug Sanders
Caroline Keggi

Betsy King
Colleen Walker
Lloyd Mangrum
Harry Cooper

Duffy Waldorf
Lori Garbacz
Brad Faxon
David Feherty

Famous Leo Swingers

LEO

VIRGO

August 23 – September 22

GOLFER

Your Celestial Golf Symbol
VIRGIN

*The only feminine figure in the Zodiac, you have a purity of thought and purpose
that can make your golf game something special for others to behold and learn from.
You and fellow Virgo, Arnold Palmer, have a way with golf
that the rest of us only dream about!*

Your Golf Element
EARTH

*When it comes to doing golf in the simplest, most practical,
whatever-swing-works-for-you way, nobody does it better than
the down-to-earth Virgo player.
We're talking the methodical assembly of a golf swing to produce
verifiable results for tangible gains. It may not always be pretty, but it works.*

Your Planetary Golf Guru
MERCURY

*This Winged Messenger of the Golf Gods gives you the mental toughness
to stay the course and keep your head on straight
when others are spinning out of control - and out of bounds.*

*Your Mercury allows you to immediately examine the mess
you've gotten yourself into, organize the most practical shot out of the mess
and then execute it with the precision of the golf craftsman and woman you are.*

VIRGO

Identifying the Virgo Golfer

The first hole. You wait your turn to tee off, re-adjusting the velcro patch on the back of your glove to just the right snugness. You remove a ball from your pocket and study the dimple configuration. You check the scorecard for the listed yardage for the hole, then look to see if the actual tee blocks have been placed forward of the marker or pushed way back. It's your turn to play, but you can't just walk up and stick your tee in the ground anywhere. No, you pace back and forth across the earth between the tee blocks, feeling for the most level, solid spot of ground to plant your feet and hit your first drive.

The foursome waiting to tee off behind you looks at each other and sighs: "Got to be a Virgo..."

You hit a good-looking drive down the fairway, but the ball does not have the specific flight pattern you have worked so hard to achieve. Because it's left of center, your next shot will be a lot tougher than if you were shooting at the pin from the right. You are now into one of the best parts of your golf game. Worry.

Worry comes so naturally and effortlessly to you that you don't always show what's really going on inside. Considering all the worry within, your eyes can still sparkle with intelligence and clarity. Your face is not a window into the critical, punctilious player you truly are.

"What other people may find in poetry or art museums,
I find in the flight of a good drive."
ARNOLD PALMER

VIRGO

Portrait of the Female Virgo Golfer

When it comes to golf, your relationship is anything but chaste and virginal. You have probably cheated on the game, had an affair with tennis, or perhaps even run off for a few hot and heavy years with the triathlon. If you ever do find something more satisfying than golf, you'll give the game the old heave-ho faster than an out-of-bounds husband.

No one plays in a more organized and efficient manner than you do. You are never late for a tee-time and woe to the foursome ahead who does not keep the pace up, for you will gladly let them know the error of their ways.

As an Earth sign, a good deal of your attraction to golf comes from your love of nature. Trees, grass and flowers help soften your ever-lurking irritation with the game.

You learned early never to blame yourself for anything that happens to you on the golf course. It's always the fault of the ball, your club, the course architect, the wind... anything and anybody but you.

Anyone who is both completely practical and utterly romantic is not about to let golf make them wrong.

Portrait of the Male Virgo Golfer

Never take your Virgin symbol too literally. When it comes to golf, your earthy ball-beating appetites are anything but innocent. Nevertheless, there is purity in your love of work, practice and discipline. You have an unselfish desire to share those qualities with less fortunate golfers. Your practical side keeps you engrossed in practice for performance sake and material gain - be it a friendly side bet or a business relationship better conducted on the course than in the boardroom.

Any lack of natural talent for golf is more than compensated for by your organized, disciplined approach to the game.

The way you play golf may not be pretty, but you get the job done.

How Virgo Plays the Mind Game

You can be a scratch player in the "mind game" of golf a lot easier than in the physical game.

Your curiosity about how things work and your determination to fix them makes it easier for you to practice long hours and stay focused where others tend to let their minds take a hike long before the ball-beating is done.

How Virgo Plays the Physical Game

A dedicated student of the game's mechanics, you are willing to work hard enough to see practical and measurable results from your practice program.

You are not a loosy goosey player with a big wild swing. Your swing is a practical working mechanism with as few moving parts as possible - all the easier to control and master. And you have the endurance to keep swinging until you do master it!

VIRGO

Best Part of the Virgo Game

You have an enormous capacity for enjoying long hours on the practice range. You can put up with more hard work on your game far longer than almost any other player. And because of your highly critical and quick mind, you are beating balls with a clear plan for specific performance enhancement.

Traps'n Hazards

You can get so caught up in your own thinking that you don't listen to what anyone else has to say who may be of real help! Objective, critical analysis of your swing is hard for you to take. And you can worry yourself into illness with too much practice and not enough play.

All work and no play makes you too cool and calculating for your own golfing good.

Perfect Foursome

You feel comfortable sharing your time with the realistic, pragmatic Capricorn. Your opposite sign of Pisces has an energy that warms something in you. And who better than Gemini to share great conversations about the whys and wherefores of the game.

Ideal Golf Courses

You are at your best on courses that come straight at you. No goofy hazards, blind man's bluff traps, or tricked-up fairways for you.

The **Blue Monster** at Doral is long and bad, but not for Virgo Ray Floyd who has won the Doral Open three times.

And **Royal Dornoch** in Scotland has something very special to offer Virgo - a good time. After playing 54 holes in a 24-hour period, fellow Virgo Tom Watson gave this critique: "This is the most fun I've had playing golf!"

Fun and golf for Virgo??

Now that's something special. More often than not you relate to a course that rewards a determined, uniquely-crafted and tightly focused golf game. The following should give you a good workout:

* **Riviera Country Club,** Los Angeles, California
* **Cherry Hills,** Inglewood, Colorado
* **Shinnecock Hills,** Southhampton, New York
* **Winged Foot,** *West,* Mamaroneck, New York
* **Colonial,** Cordova, Tennessee
* **Bay Hill,** Orlando, Florida
* **La Costa,** Carlsbad, California
* **Butler National,** Oak Brook, Illinois
* **Turnberry Golf Club,** Scotland
* **Muirfield Village Golf Club,** Dublin, Ohio
* **Laurel Valley Golf Club,** Ligonier, Pennsylvania
* **Royal Birkdale,** Southport, England
* **Pasatiempo,** Santa Cruz, California

Best Colors to Wear While Playing

Because you are as critical about how you look as how you think and work, your golfing attire has to be just so - conservative rather than flashy - but everything in it's place.

You work best in gray, beige and all shades of green. Cool jade, navy blue, platinum and even pure white compliment and symbolize your purity of purpose and thought.

Shooting Stars for Shooting Pars

* *Spend more time thinking about what went right than what went wrong. What you think is what you get. So stop thinking UGLY!*

* *You don't have to figure everything out and fix everything before you can enjoy playing golf.*

* *Get in touch with that quiet, shy Virgo child inside who wants to have fun. It's not more golf you need to play, it's more play you need to get into your golf!*

The Virgo Senior Swinger

Now's the time to let go of your intense work ethic and allow yourself a play ethic.

Your critical, worrisome mind has worked hard enough. Give it time off for good behavior. Put that practical, precise, painstaking, problem-solving, pessimist on parole!

You have always had a great sense of humor. Use it now more than ever. Be willing to lighten up, and you will warm up to these golden golfing years.

Your Personal Fairways to the Glory of Golf

*   *Make time to play when you can enjoy the quiet peace and beauty of being on the golf course alone. Then send your doubting, analytical mind to camp, put trust in your gut, and play for the pure pleasure of playing. People who get fully involved in playing always accomplish more than golfers who try too hard.*

*   *Why waste time worrying about your screwups? Allow yourself the luxury of failure. Only a mediocre golfer is always at his best.*

*   *Because you are such a worker, a nit-picker and a perfectionist, you can't help but take your golf performance seriously. It is much easier for you to be serious than frivolous. Lighten up, and your handicap will hunker down.*

*   *In golf there is understanding from the head, believing from the heart, and knowing from the soul. You've got the first one. Get the next two and you will become the player you wish to be.*

VIRGO

Virgo
Uncensored

"I never had a good bounce. All I ever had were bad ones."
ARNOLD PALMER

"The game was easy for me as a kid,
and I had to play awhile to find out how hard it is."
RAY FLOYD

"Did you ever smell your golf bag
after you carried a tuna sandwich around in the hot sun?"
AL GEIBERGER

"It takes so long to accept that you can't always
replicate your swing. The only thing you can control
is your attitude toward the next shot."
MARK McCUMBER

"The person I fear most in the last two rounds is myself."
TOM WATSON

Arnold Palmer
Isao Aoki
Larry Nelson
Cindy Rarick

Jane Blalock
Jeff Sluman
Mark McCumber
Al Geiberger

Ray Floyd
Chip Beck
Bernard Langer
Louise Suggs

Tom Watson
David Frost
Scott Simpson
Lee Janzen

Famous Virgo Swingers

VIRGO

LIBRA

September 23 – October 22

GOLFER

Your Celestial Golf Symbol

SCALES

Harmony, peace, and balance in all aspects of the game rule your enjoyment of golf. For you, great golf is achieving a perfect balance in all the challenges and disciplines the game has to offer. Whether between high-tech and tradition in your equipment, mechanics versus feel in your swing, or the mind game versus the physical game, you strive for an aesthetic and harmonious balance.

Your Golf Element

AIR

As the second Air Sign, your relationship with golf is like a marriage. You and the game have made a pledge to play together, for richer or poorer, in sickness and in health, for better or for worse.

Your Planetary Golf Guru

VENUS

You can thank your lucky Venus, who enables you to smile when golf does its best to break your heart. This Goddess not only fills you with love, but makes you lovable to others for the bright, colorful and unique talent you bring to the game. Because Venus rules the heart and throat, you are blessed with the ability to express your wonderful thoughts on golf as warmly as you feel them inside.

Identifying the Libra Golfer

Though you seek balance in your golf swing, finding it is another matter. You are ever in search of that new piece of instruction or equipment which promises to get you back to center.

Your need for balance comes from feeling so little of it within yourself. Libras tend to seek the very thing they lack. You can be cheerful and bright on the front nine and sulk your way down the backside. You're able to mediate any penalties and/or rules infractions with liberty and justice for all on one hole, yet have no trouble putting up a good argument for your own rights according to the book on the next.

You have the wonderful talent to walk your talk. But you also listen, hear, and consider the truth of what any playing partners have to say. It is this unique ability to walk both sides of the fairway that amazes others and can be frustrating to you. How do you know which side is the best?

For you, golf is an art form. You are the painter and the course your canvas. As unique and often ungainly as your brush strokes can be, you are still able to produce scenes and shots of great beauty. You can be all over the canvas, but eventually it all comes together and Libra is at peace and harmony with the heavenly game.

"Golf is an awkward set of bodily contortions
designed to produce a graceful result."
TOMMY ARMOUR

LIBRA

Portrait of the Female Libra Golfer

You are so charming and persuasive and your positions on everything about the game are presented with such diplomacy that it's hard for anyone not to be swayed.

The tough part for you is that just about everything in golf is open for debate. How can you possibly not argue the merits of oversize clubheads versus the aesthetics of a traditional blade or the merits of putting on bentgrass versus Bermuda?

You argue both sides of any golf question so intelligently and fairly that you can be a most entertaining spectator sport for others to enjoy from the sidelines.

You are one of those rare signs that enjoy teeing it up with the guys as comfortably as playing with women friends. You can talk the game's hardware, software, and underwear, but rarely let the guys know you know more than they do.

With your affinity for the harmony of sound, color and use of words, you need a teacher who is not only a golf pro, but also a poet and artist in communicating the best swing for you.

Portrait of the Male Libra Golfer

Getting ready to play is your biggest handicap. You need to make the right decision which means you may spend more time deciding what to wear, whom to take lessons from, what equipment to buy and which driving range to practice on, than you spend playing the game!

For Libra, more than any other sign, golf is a team sport. You need and want all the support you can get - from your partner, your caddie, even your golf cart - anyone who will listen to you. You enjoy the game more when you have a playmate. You play better in almost any partner's best-ball format than when you play alone.

Under it all, you are the gentle lover of all that's good and wholesome about golf - in spite of what you may do when your game goes out of balance.

How Libra Plays the Mind Game

To the extremes. You can easily dwell on negative thoughts which you freely verbalize to the rest of your foursome. If and when you get past the negativity, you can be just as persuasive in positive, constructive mind games that can be an enormous help to your own golf game as well as anyone still willing to listen to you.

Above all, you feel a real partnership with golf and use your mind to ensure justice and fair play for all who take club in hand in pursuit of that pocked-marked little ball.

How Libra Plays the Physical Game

Libra rarely has a natural talent for good golf posture or overall body alignment. Your grip and swing tend to be very intense rather than relaxed and flowing with the balance you are forever seeking.

While you may never have the most graceful swing, you can develop a unique swing that your mind can master and be at peace with.

LIBRA

Best Part of the Libra Game

You make a great partner in team events. Your ability to find the right compliment of qualities for optimum performance pairings makes you a great team leader, golf coach or tournament organizer.

Your loyalty to the high ideals of the game and concern for fair play make you a perfect candidate for president of your local golf club's rules committee. Your tremendous ability to weigh and reason complicated situations, and counsel others in a non-threatening way, makes you perhaps better at helping others improve their games than helping yourself.

Traps'n Hazards

You weigh the alternatives of everything so carefully that you take forever to make a decision - which can make you one of the slowest players on the course, a real double bogey, because you are forever wanting and needing approval from others.

These negative expressions show up more when you are bored playing courses that are not aesthetically pleasing or don't inspire your creative abilities. When you feel your mind, body and spirit are really out of balance, stay off the golf course. If you have no choice and have to play, let the rest of your foursome know it could be an "X-rated" game - at least on the scorecard.

Perfect Foursome

Gemini can help you make up your mind a lot faster. You have no problem being praised by Leo and don't mind playing second fiddle. And Sagittarius can certainly add some sparks to the fun and good times.

Ideal Golf Courses

You have a great appreciation for natural beauty as well as an affinity for design and form which makes the choice of courses an important decision for you. One of the greatest attractions golf has is the aesthetic nature of the game. When playing courses of exquisite beauty, you are inspired to rise above your physical limitations and become a player with an almost beautiful swing.

At the top of any such list will always be **Pebble Beach, Cypress Point, Pine Valley, Augusta** and **Pinehurst #2.**

But here are a few more courses that should have something for every Libra to love!

* **Old Ballybunion** and **Lahinch** in Ireland
* **Mauna Kea, The Prince, Kapalua,** and the **Challenge at Manelo** in Hawaii
* **Pelican Hill,** *Ocean,* Newport Coast, California
* **Four Seasons Resort Aviara,** Carlsbad, California
* **Boulders, Ventana Canyon** and **Troon,** Arizona
* **The Cliffs,** South Carolina
* **Jackson Hole Golf Club,** Wyoming
* **Pumpkin Ridge,** *Ghost Creek Course,* Cornelius, Oregon
* **Samoset Resort,** Maine
* **Black Diamond,** *Quarry Course,* Lecanto, Florida
* **Tryall Golf & Beach Club,** Jamaica
* **Les Bordes,** France

LIBRA

Best Colors to Wear While Playing

Pink, pale green and blue are the colors for you.

"Pastels and soft shades
do your golf game the best
Leave the bright hot hues
for the rest to be dressed"

Shooting Stars for Shooting Pars

* *You've got the dreams. Now expand them into strong, on course action.*

* *You are great at advising others. People listen. Perhaps you should take your own best advice.*

* *When you know and trust your intuition about what shot to play and how best to play it, your decision-making won't be so agonizing - for you or your playing partners.*

The Libra Senior Swinger

You need a connection to other golfers, so now's the time to commit yourself to some charitable organization that needs you to seek and maintain justice and equality for golfers of all handicaps.

Find a group of energetic people facing the biggest challenges, and you will rise to the occasion with the mind and body of a person half your age!

Yes, Libra, you are one of the lucky ones who rarely show your age. Somewhere in your struggles to find that perfect balance you and your body have made peace.

Your Personal Fairways to the Glory of Golf

* *To make the most out of golf, make the least out of brooding over past performance.*

* *Procrastination is the root of your golfing evils. Stop putting off a good hard look at how you play the game inside, just because you're afraid you may not like the "player" you meet.*

* *The game will never be perfect. It wasn't meant to be. Neither were you. So send your doubting mind to camp, put trust in your gut, take a whack at it, and let the chips and putts fall where they may.*

* *No matter how many ways to play a particular shot, a golf shot is still just a golf shot. Don't make it harder than it is, and you will play it easier than you think.*

* *Don't let your need for balance make your golf game dull and boring. The moments you remember are not the well plotted pars from the middle of perfect fairways, but the miraculous escapes from traps and hazards, the soaring spirit you experience from those little detours off the beaten path. That's what makes the stuff worth remembering. And that's what makes golf worth playing.*

LIBRA

Libra
Uncensored

"I'd probably be the fat lady in a circus right now
if it hadn't been for golf. It kept me on the course
and out of the refrigerator."
KATHY WHITWORTH

"In Europe, we think it's funny that Tour players travel with a
sports psychologist or call one after every round."
ERNIE ELS

"Golf is like hunting and fishing.
What counts is the companionship and fellowship of friends,
not what you catch or shoot."
GEORGE ARCHER

"As kids we were playing so much,
someone was always winning or losing. So it didn't matter.
What was important was the game.
You can have a good time and still compete."
FRED COUPLES

"If I can't win, then I won't play."
LAURA DAVIES

Kathy Whitworth
Bruce Devlin
Sally Little
Ernie Els

Fred Couples   Tommy Armour
Beth Daniel   Vicki Goetz
Harold Henning   Larry Mize
Gil Morgan   Val Skinner

Laura Davies
George Archer
Sherri Turner
John Cook

Famous Libra Swingers

LIBRA

SCORPIO

October 23 – November 21

GOLFER

Your Celestial Golf Symbol

SCORPION/EAGLE

*You may already know about the sting of your tail, but did you know that
your symbol is also the Eagle! What better image to represent your ability
to rise above golf's traps and hazards and achieve your greatest potential.*

*Because the Scorpion and Eagle are related to life and death,
you can shed the pain and negativity of poor performance - let go of the past -
and give birth to a fresh, exciting new game the next time you tee it up.*

Your Golf Element

WATER

*Your water element can be a deep, dark hazard where you hide a good part of
your passion for the game. Your deepest feelings about the game
may seem so outrageous that you'd rather keep them secret.
But sharing your insights, no matter how unusual or bizarre,
helps others generate more passion for the game you love so much.*

Your Planetary Golf Guru

MARS & PLUTO

*Mars, God of War, gives you the passion and the staying power to rise to
every challenge golf presents, and play as though each round were your last.*

*Pluto belongs to the underworld of volcanoes and earthquakes,
beginnings and endings, and to the creative forces.
What is the game more about
than earthquakes of the stomach and soul?*

*With Mars and Pluto as your Gurus, you have the inner strength, fighting spirit,
and power of regeneration to rise above disaster and keep swinging.*

Identifying the Scorpio Golfer

Since Scorpios like to play in disguise, you are perhaps the toughest of all signs to detect.

You know who you are as a golfer and who you're not. You don't need anyone else's compliments to let you know you hit a "great shot." Criticism rolls off your backswing just as easily. You know when your golf's been good, or bad, and satisfying your own ego is all that's necessary.

You sizzle and throw off sparks when you golf. You may try to be cool and loose like Scorpio Fuzzy Zoeller, but no one can hide such an energy force completely. Just ask Patty Sheehan or Tom Weiskopf.

Your powerful lust for the links is not only expressed in your physical connection to the game, but in how you choose to perceive this unrequited golf affair.

If your golf passion is unfulfilled, your dark side may express itself in wild, overheated swinging, lost weekends at La Costa, and acute ball-beating dependency! For Scorpio, that may be as good as it gets.

"I was afraid to move my lips in front of TV. They probably would have fined me for what I was thinking."
TOM WEISKOPF

SCORPIO

Portrait of the Female Scorpio Golfer

Fasten your seat belts and bag strap because you're in for a bumpy ride!

When you play golf, you mean business. You see no need to be coy about the way you hit the ball or play the game. You may try to hide your hard-core ball-beating behind a quiet voice and sweet smile, but if anyone can seduce a golf course and have her way with it it is you.

You can overpower the course on the frontside and melt it into submission on the back. You may twist and shout, shriek and wail your frustration and loathing for the game's transgressions, then, with the blink of an eye, find yourself purring to your driver, which has seen the error of its ways and will never stray from the straight and narrow again.

Your love affair with golf ranks right up there with the passionate affairs of your sister Scorpios, Grace Kelly, Katherine Hepburn, Vivien Leigh and Marie Antoinette!

Portrait of the Male Scorpio Golfer

A passion for golf? Yes. A passion for food, work, clothing, and all the finer things in life fills your soul to overflowing. "More is better" is your mantra.

Then how do you play with such self-control? With all that's bubbling inside you, you have a sureness of purpose and a strong need to maintain dignity in your game.

You value your own judgments over those of others. You'd like others to respect your game, but far more important is living up to the high standards you've set for yourself.

You need and seek the truth about what golf really is. A free spirit or loose cannon, once your passion is aroused, golf is a lifetime affair. The game itself, with all its physical, emotional and fantasy possibilities has the seductive mystery and slightly sinful attraction of making eye contact with a beautiful stranger across a crowded room. You can't help moving your feet toward the first tee!

How Scorpio Plays the Mind Game

You play the mental game as intensely as the physical one. Your powers of concentration are frightening. Playing your own secret little game on that six-inch course between your ears, you are out to lunch as far as anyone else in your foursome is concerned.

The depth of your thinking can also be your downfall. You can too easily get lost in the esoteric, psychological and meta-physical interpretations of golf that are so seductive to the Scorpio intellect.

How Scorpio Plays the Physical Game

Your intensity is reflected in nervous mannerisms; lots of club waggling and wiggling of the feet at address. Some of that passionate energy can be safely released through walking the course. If forced to ride a golf cart, your tension may be released in your golf swing, which can easily fly out of control.

Your swing tends to be studied and calculated. Anything you can do to relax and let your body smoothly release through the shot is critical for Scorpio success.

SCORPIO

Best Part of the Scorpio Game

Your determination, powers of concentration, great imagination, and love of the challenge golf provides make you a passionate player.

No one has to tell you how to play a particular shot. And you need no one's approval but your own. Your golf game is not defined by what anyone else thinks.

Traps'n Hazards

Your very strength is your weakness. You are so self-contained that you have difficulty taking advice or criticism - no matter how beneficial to your game.

Because you take such complete responsibility for everything that happens on the course, you can really beat yourself up for poor performance. And you are no more forgiving of others. Which means you may eventually lose a few playing partners... perhaps even yourself.

Perfect Foursome

Leo's ego is almost as big as yours and you can play with that. You get hooked on Sagittarius' high flying optimism. And you love Aries' energy and gusto for playing the game.

(Actually, you'd be just as happy playing with a threesome of Scorpios, too wrapped up in their own games to bother you - rather like playing alone, which also works just fine.)

Ideal Golf Courses

Any course that's magnificent enough to give your passionate ego a game worth playing.

Plain layouts that are easy to score on bore you. They don't hold your interest long enough to keep your mind and swing from wandering. You need exceptional courses with a brooding, dangerous mystique.

Bali Handara Country Club in Bali was made for Scorpio. Located in the midst of an extinct volcano, the beauty of the valley is sure to ignite Scorpio's passion for the game.

But for the ultimate Scorpio experience you must go to France and play at **Golfs du Chateau de La Salle,** where the entire course has been modeled on a woman's body. Every curve, every swale and mound is a replica of some feature of Nicole Jobert. From ankle to neck, every nuance of her physique has been celebrated in the course design.

With Nicole Jobert to test your Scorpio golf appetites, you may have met your match. To play passionately on this course is to play all the shots from rough to bunkers and be so infatuated with the whole affair that you don't care how many strokes it takes!

Now all you Scorpio women need is someone to design a course around the body of Arnold Schwarzenegger.

A few other courses Scorpio may want to seduce:

* **PGA West,** *Stadium,* LaQuinta, California
* **Kiawah Island,** *Ocean Course,* South Carolina
* **Casa de Campo, Teeth of the Dog,** La Romana, Dominican Republic
* **Troon, North,** Scottsdale, Arizona
* **Royal Troon Golf Club,** Scotland
* **Shadow Glen Golf Course,** Olathe, Kansas
* **TPC at Sawgrass,** *Stadium,* Ponte Vedra Beach, Florida
* **Forest Highlands,** Flagstaff, Arizona
* **Spyglass Hill,** Pebble Beach, California

Best Colors to Wear While Playing

Life and death. Strong contrasting colors. Red with black. Reddish orange, deep crimson, Magenta and wine will ground you to your golf source.

Soft, subdued tones are contrary to your nature, but may help balance the nervous energy attacking your set-up and pre-shot routine.

Shooting Stars for Shooting Pars

*   *Play from your heart. Let your ego be your caddie.*

*   *Balance your dark side with a passionate belief in yourself and your game will be more rewarding than ever.*

*   *Pace yourself. Don't use up all that intensity and passion before you get to the last three holes.*

The Scorpio Senior Swinger

Golf is the perfect outlet for you in later years. It's the one place where it's okay not to be a grown up, serious adult.

You can be a kid again. You don't have to play that heavy, intellectual mind game to play your best golf. The dark, secretive side of you has had its day and now you can let go of that and just play golf. You've already discovered that growing up can be hell on your handicap. Now you've got the whole back nine to play!

Learn the truth of the words of that all-time classic swinger, Plato, who said, "Life must be lived as play."

Now golf must be played to live!

Your Personal Fairways to the Glory of Golf

* *The kundolini energy, or sexual force, that lies at the bottom of the spine can be used to ignite a single-mindedness of passion to carry you beyond your normal physical abilities. Use your sexuality to transform yourself and play golf in the "zone."*

* *You will find more joy in golf and play better when you get out of your dark spiked soul. Enjoy the company of other golfers. Their companionship may turn out to be worthy of your attention.*

* *With the Scorpion and the Eagle at your side, you possess the power and will to rise above the crowd. How you choose to get there - with a deadly sting from your Scorpion tail, or on your Eagle's wings - is up to you.*

* *Golf introduces a person to himself or herself. The best you can hope for is to like that person you meet.*

SCORPIO

Scorpio Uncensored

"I've quit worrying about poor shots.
I just tell myself, 'Relax, Bozo.
If you can't have fun, you shouldn't be out here.'"
PATTY SHEEHAN

"The way I hit the ball today, I need to go to the range.
Instead, I think I'll go to the bar."
FUZZY ZOELLER

"It's a marriage.
If I had to choose between my wife and my putter...
Well, I'd miss her."
GARY PLAYER

"I would like to knock it on every green and two-putt,
but that's not my style of play or my style of living."
MUFFIN SPENCER-DEVLIN

"I'm gonna be a firecracker out there today. I'm gonna be so
hot they're gonna be playing on brown fairways tomorrow."
CHI CHI RODRIQUEZ

Corey Pavin
Debbie Massey
Gary Player
Bobby Locke

Patty Sheehan
Ian Baker-Finch
Joyce Wethered
Dave Stockton

Fuzzy Zoeller
Muffin Spencer-Devlin
Tommy Nakajima
Don January

Chi Chi Rodriquez
Barbara Romack
Peggy Kirk Bell
Tom Weiskopf

Famous Scorpio Swingers

SCORPIO

SAGITTARIVS

SAGITTARIUS

November 22 – December 21

GOLFER

Your Celestial Golf Symbol
THE CENTAUR

Half man and half horse, the archer ever shooting toward heavenly golf, that's you!
You know the secrets of the game and feel a duty to minister to the needs of innocent
men, women, and children who suffer the game's frustration and humiliation.

Your Golf Element
FIRE

With fire as your element, you have the capacity to encourage and inspire other players,
and the charisma to lead others on the great adventure that golf can be.
Your energy, encouragement and good humor fairly bubble as you are driven
to explore and expand the game by example.

Your Planetary Golf Guru
JUPITER

Another name for Jupiter was Jove, the source of the word "jovial."
Is it any wonder you have such a bright and happy personality?

To have the planet of good fortune as your guide enables you to smile
in the face of disaster. What happens to you on the course doesn't matter
as much as how you react to it. With your ability to see the potential for success
and victory in even the worst of circumstances, you are a tough act to follow -
and even tougher to beat.

Jupiter fills you with the absolute certainty that you can and will achieve your desires.
Jupiter is also the protector of justice and virtue.
Add the qualities of wisdom and optimism, and you become
a powerful presence on the golf course.

Identifying the Sagittarius Golfer

It's not hard to spot you on the course. You entertain whoever is in earshot, passing out wit and wisdom on the more esoteric qualities of golf, while oblivious to the rake you are about to step on, sending the handle on a perfect drive for the center of your head.

Later, at the 19th hole bar, the rake incident will inspire a story of perseverance overcoming knucklehead stupidity and have everyone enthralled, hanging on for the big finish which may include a sweeping flourish of an arm accidentally hitting the sweet spot of a passing cocktail waitress. "No harm, no foul!" you plead to one and all. An honest mistake in body mechanics and spatial judgment. You would never do such a thing knowingly.

And you're right. Deception and pretense are not part of your game plan. But perpetual motion is. You do not operate well at a slow idle. Your confidence makes you anxious to get on with the game.

You are also golf's resident dare-devil. The inherent risk/reward nature of the game really lights your fire. You're going to shoot yourself in the foot now and then, but one of these times you know it's going to be a hole-in-one!

Once you have seen what golf can be and what it will take to get it, you saddle up your high horse, fill your quiver with your own unique brand of arrows and gallop of into the wonderful world of "fore-play."

Nobody plays it more entertainingly and passionately than Sagittarius.

"When you talk as fast as I do, you can't choose your words.
Whatever flies into my head, I say.
Believe me, I've eaten my share of tennis shoes as a result."
LEE TREVINO

SAGITTARIUS

Portrait of the Female Sagittarius Golfer

Doris Day movies may have gone out with the 1960's, but not you. Then again, your perfect Pollyanna image can be easily shattered when you say what's on your mind. No harm intended. You just can't tell a lie.

If your golf friends aren't strong enough to put up with your outspoken frankness, that's their loss.

And though you'll probably make a joke of it, you can be heartbroken that someone you enjoy playing with could have possibly been hurt when you suggested she might help your team more by not taking five minutes to read the break on every two-foot putt and just knock the damn ball in the hole!

Is it really necessary for you to explain that if she just relaxed, took aim and stroked the ball, she'd make it a lot easier on herself?

Of course that's what you meant! Do you have to spell out everything?!

Portrait of the Male Sagittarius Golfer

When you think Sagittarius, think Walter Hagen, Lee Trevino and Lanny Wadkins. You are out there all over the place and make the game better for us all. Your enthusiasm and curiosity for golf knows no bounds - like some of your shots, particularly the verbal shots you take at the game and those who attempt to play it.

You don't mean to hurt feelings, but when a brilliant, insightful gem of wisdom pops into your head, how can you not share it with the rest of your foursome, or the crowd that is often around you? Your optimism for everything golf can be is contagious and honey for the rest of us who expect the worst from our golf - and accomplish it admirably!

How Sagittarius Plays the Mind Game

To quote Walter Hagen, "Give me a man with big hands, big feet, and no brains, and I'll make a golfer out of him!"

Which is not to say you don't think your way around the course. But like your symbol, the half-man, half-horse Centaur, you probably feel you only need half a mind to play your best golf.

Oh, you can wax philosophical about the nature of golf, but your intuition, ingenuity and instincts play a far bigger role in your ability than a great deal of intense, analytical thinking.

For Sagittarius...

"Overthinking can be stinking
to the shot you've just defined
For the longer you take to think
become the shots that
drive you to drink
To play your best, it helps
to be out of your mind."

How Sagittarius Plays the Physical Game

There is nothing shy or reserved about your swing or the way you stride down the fairway. You are bigger than life and your swinging arms and long striding gait make you easy to spot in the middle of the gallery that you seem to attract.

While you tend to have strong muscles in your hands and feet, you can be clumsy with smaller objects such as balls and tees. Your typically stout torso is well suited to golf and you show no caution in throwing your body and soul into the game.

Sagittarius is as physically fit as Rocky Balboa. No matter how the game beats you down, you're ready to come back for one more round - on and off the course!

SAGITTARIVS

Best Part of the Sagittarius Game

Your bottomless well of enthusiasm and optimism allows you to take full advantage of the luck you seem to fall into on any fairway. You love the game and all the finer things life has to offer. You refuse to be discouraged by some of the not so finer traps and hazards awaiting us all. This is what sets you apart from the crowd.

As it was said about Sagittarian, Lanny Wadkins, "He's the kind of optimist who, if he falls in the sewer, checks his pockets for fish!"

Traps'n Hazards

Does false pride, overconfidence and shooting for the moon, or shooting your mouth off, get you in trouble? Without patience for details, and focus on the end result, you may find all too much in common with the rhyme:

"I shot an arrow (excuse me) a golf ball into the air, and where it landed, I knew not where."

While you would never be deliberately cruel, your mouth can get you into more trouble than your worst shank. Your honesty can be too forthright for some over-sensitive golfers who may not share your inherent sportsmanship.

Just because you are hell-bent to swing it your way, as sure as that Sagittarius of song, Mr. Sinatra sings it his way, don't let your rebellious spirit detract from the good that conformity has to offer.

Perfect Foursome

You admire Aries' fire and spirit for the game. Aquarius' cool and detached nature can have its advantages. And social golf with Libra can be great fun and a playing lesson in the value of better balance and harmony.

Ideal Golf Courses

Anywhere the action is! For you it may be a question of who is playing as much as the course they're playing on. Your outgoing personality and bigger than life approach to the game thrive on playing with other high-flying personalities.

A few rounds in Las Vegas suits you to a tee, particularly **Shadow Creek Golf Club**. The gambler in you will love **The Legacy** where the four tee boxes on the par 3, 10th hole are shaped like the four suits in a deck of cards: diamonds, hearts, clubs and spades.

Bel Air Country Club deep in the heart of Beverly Hills has all the famous and celebrated swingers you could ever hope to play a round with.

Then take a limo out to Thousand Oaks and **Sherwood Country Club** where Jack Nicholson and the gang get it on.

And the Palm Springs area has enough golf courses, celebrities and action to keep your mind and mouth motoring merrily along.

* **La Quinta Hotel Golf Club,** La Quinta, California
* **Big Horn,** Palm Desert, California
* **Indian Wells Golf Resort,** Indian Wells, California

A few more courses worthy of your time and money:

* **Edgewood Tahoe,** Lake Tahoe, Nevada
* **Riviera Country Club,** Pacific Palisades, California
* **San Francisco Golf Course,** San Francisco, California
* **Seminole Golf Course,** North Palm Beach, Florida
* **Valderama, Spain,** the "Augusta National" of Europe
* **Las Brises,** Spain
* **Mauna Lani Resort,** Big Island, Hawaii

SAGITTARIUS

Best Colors to Wear While Playing

Since purple relates to spiritual enlightenment, it can be a highly energizing color for you. The specific garments you wear undoubtedly will be as unique as your entire approach to golf.

Other colors that may add to your aura include magenta, amethyst and deep blue.

Shooting Stars for Shooting Pars

* *What is on your mind is often too quick on your lips. Get a good grip before you let it rip from the lip!*

* *Temper your high energy gregariousness with a more modest, warmer approach to the "short game."*

* *To achieve your ultimate goals, you need a connection between body, mind and spirit. It is too easy for you to play with the body and leave the other two buried in the bag.*

The Sagittarius Senior Swinger

For you growing older has nothing to do with getting old. Old you'll never be. Older is just a little slower and a little wiser. Time to travel more, meet other exciting players, and savor "the time in-between."

You may begin teaching and writing about golf. Let your philosophical side stretch. You will not only be more tolerant of other's ways to play the game, but will no longer be so adamant that yours is unquestionably "the way" to the glory of golf.

Your Personal Fairways to the Glory of Golf

* *Just because you have enough self-assurance to attain most of your golfing desires doesn't mean you have to also achieve the dreams of your golfing friends!*

* *Realize that not everybody is on the same fairway. Some of your friends are not even playing the same course! Give them a break and ease off on the right way to swing, putt and play cards.*

* *The fact that you are genuinely hurt when your direct honesty wounds another's heart or handicap may be not enough to heal the hurt. Not everyone wants to know the truth... Yourself included!*

* *Judgment is the key. Rely too much on good fortune to get you out of every trap and hazard and you may run out of luck long before you run out of golf.*

* *Never stop aiming for those unreachable pars in the stars, but don't be blind to the joy and beauty that's within your reach everyday.*

SAGITTARIUS

Sagittarius Uncensored

"I never wanted to be a millionaire,
I just wanted to live like one!"
WALTER HAGEN

"My family have been farmers for generations.
They are overjoyed that people actually call me 'Dirt'."
BRAD BRYANT
"Dr. Dirt"

"I don't like being average. I'm out here to win tournaments."
TAMMY GREEN

"I'm not in awe of anybody. Never have been.
I'm not gonna be intimidated. I refuse to be."
LANNY WADKINS

"My dear, did you ever stop to think what a lovely
bunker you would make?"
WALTER HAGEN
(to a famous opera singer!)

Lee Trevino
Ralph Guldahl
Jane Fonda
Tom Kite

Lanny Wadkins
Scott Hoch
Jay Haas
Rocco Mediate

Steve Elkington
Tom Purtzer
Brad Bryant
Shirley Englehorn

Tammy Green
Danielle Ammaccapane
Betty Grable
Walter Hagen

Famous Sagittarius Swingers

SAGITTARIUS

CAPRICORN

CAPRICORN

December 22 – January 19

GOLFER

Your Celestial Golf Symbol
MOUNTAIN GOAT

*It comes as no surprise that you want to climb to the peak of your golfing potential.
You get bored with flat courses, and relish the challenge of layouts with mountains
and cliffs - courses that humiliate other, less surefooted signs.*

Your Golf Element
EARTH

*You feel particularly connected to the ground you play upon.
You have always had good footwork in your swing and know intuitively that
golf is played from the ground up. The Earth's energy radiates up through your soles
into your legs, generating the power for your swing.*

Your Planetary Golf Guru
SATURN

*Saturday comes from Saturn and is a great golf day for you.
As your in-house pro, Saturn teaches you endurance,
patience and above all, self-discipline.
Saturn is also the "time-keeper." Part of the self-discipline you need most
is to know when it's time to give the game a rest.*

*Add the qualities of wisdom and optimism, and you become
a powerful presence on the golf course.*

Identifying the Capricorn Golfer

You don't always look like the player you are. Perhaps slow and deliberate, you know what the score is, and you know a round of golf is eighteen holes. Your patience and persistence usually pays off around the 19th hole.

You prefer to play with almost boring consistency, watching the flashy players rip it all over the map and go from birdie to bust.

No one gives you a shot against the big hitters and scratch wanna-be's, yet you usually win. And no one can figure it. You don't look that good. You don't look like a "player." But your persistent, plodding, one shot at a time, one hole at a time game plan adds up to a powerful golfing presence.

You also have a strong attraction to the "perks" that go with the territory. Do you golf for the love of it? Or for the business deals, money and social status it can give you?

Acknowledge this attraction, then putt out and move on.

Dependable, loyal and dedicated to the game, you are also practical enough to be the one in your group who schedules tee-times and handles the "down to Earth" details to ensure a good golfing time is had by all.

"Man, I've got to blow dry my hair... I don't play anywhere unless I can blow dry my hair."
BEN CRENSHAW

CAPRICORN

Portrait of the Female Capricorn Golfer

You can be a serious single-digit swinger or a 32-handicap happy hacker. But what you want and need most from your golfing is recognition and respect.

If that comes from beating other players, you will do what you have to do. Or if you seek the security of your group and greater authority within it, you'll climb that particular par 5 and receive your acclaim - no matter how many strokes it takes!

If your golfing friends make fun of you, or you are too belittled by the game itself, you may walk away from golf for weeks and possibly months at a time. On balance though, at whatever level you choose to play, you will do it with great dignity, even temper and quiet grace.

Portrait of the Male Capricorn Golfer

You are self-contained and a perfectionist. Golf can drive you crazy.

Your tendency is to do whatever it takes to climb to the top of the game. Whatever the cost - in lessons, equipment, greens fees - there's a part of you that will sell the farm and mortgage the kids to climb that fairway to the unreachable par!

But you are also realistic and sensible. That, along with your wicked sense of humor, keeps your "golf-dependency" balanced enough so you don't go completely out of bounds.

You know the game is played inside out, but you have a difficult time turning your insides out there for others to see.

You are a player who loves the beauty and sensory pleasures of the game. One who loves to stop and smell the roses. But because of Saturn's discipline, you will keep your calm, cool, calculating cover and rarely show your true golfaholic lust for the game.

How Capricorn Plays the Mind Game

You have a strong, powerful mind and are capable of staying focused for eighteen holes. Because you make plans and stick to them, you are not as open to changing your game plan in the middle of a round - even if Plan "A" isn't working.

You take a long-term view of the game. Over the long haul you know what works best for you. You are not going to change for the sake of the short-term.

When it comes to improvising - even when you're on the spot and the game hangs in the balance - you'd rather dance with the partner you brung to the first tee.

How Capricorn Plays the Physical Game

You are built for the long haul. A thirty-six hole day of matchplay? Works for you!

You are agile - if not always graceful. Your arms and legs are your best body parts and your swing should stress strong leg action and supple flowing arms through impact. Don't let your controlling mind restrict and tighten your swing.

CAPRICORN

Best Part of the Capricorn Game

You are blessed with the patience to practice and hone every part of your game. Your dedication to achieving your golf dream is second to none.

You are a ball-beating machine and neither wind, rain, sleet, nor dark of night keep you from your appointed tee times. Your persistence and plodding determination to climb that path to peak performance is unsurpassed. For Capricorn golfers, "slow and steady" wins the match.

Traps'n Hazards

You don't know when to give it a rest! For yourself and everyone else who has to put up with your die-hard, ball-beating behavior.

If you don't lighten up, your Saturn makes it all too easy for you to get down on your game, until golf becomes four to five hours of humiliating self-abuse, doom and gloom.

Perfect Foursome

You like the sensible and earthy nature of Taurus. Virgo's perfection makes you feel you're not alone in your quest for the perfect golf swing.

Tee it up with another Capricorn and it's a "golfaholic" mutual admiration society - and a formidable team for anyone else to beat.

Ideal Golf Courses

Tee it up at **Crans-sur-Sierre** in the Berner Alps of Switzerland and you're a happy climber. Encircled by spectacular snow-capped peaks, the course has held seven Swiss Opens.

And you have what it takes to scale **Breckenridge Golf Club** in Colorado. Chiselled into the Continental Divide at 9,300 feet only locals and Capricorn swingers acclimated to the altitude are able to walk the course.

Tighten your spikes when you reach the par 5, 15th hole at **Peppermill Palms** in Mesquite, Nevada. The tee box is 1,114 feet higher than the fairway!

Your connection to the Earth is not related solely to the mountains, but also to the valleys. Head for Death Valley, California, and tee it down at the world's lowest golf course, 214 feet below sea level, **Furnace Creek Golf Course**. From coyotes to geese, wildlife abounds – but you won't if you play it in the summer.

But you haven't really arrived at the pinnacle of golf until you've played the **Royal Nepal Golf Club,** where on a clear day you can see Mount Everest!

Other Capricorn friendly courses include:

* **The Resort at Squaw Creek,** Squaw Valley, California
* **The Lodge at Cordillera,** Colorado
* **Makaelei,** Kona, Hawaii
* **Castle Pines,** Colorado
* **Kananaskis County Golf Course,** Alberta, Canada
* **The Lodge at Cloudcroft,** New Mexico
* **Broken Top,** Bend, Oregon
* **Plantation Course, Kapalua Golf Club,** Maui, Hawaii
* **The Broadmoor Golf Club,** Colorado Springs, Colorado

CAPRICORN

Best Colors to Wear While Playing

Your golf wardrobe is a veritable rainbow of earth colors: dark green, black and dark brown. The staunch practicality of brown keeps you and your golf game on solid ground.

Shooting Stars for Shooting Pars

* *It is better to be an optimist and be thought a fool, than be a pessimist and be right!*
* *"Work hard, play hard" may be the mantra for today's workaholic. But for you, "play hard" just makes golf hard to play! Play "easy" and you may actually have FUN on the golf course.*
* *Levity leads to longevity – on and off the golf course playground*

The Capricorn Senior Swinger

Finally, all that hard work and practice to reach the top of our game pays off. Now you can ease up and enjoy playing - perhaps even more than when you had to prove something.

If you haven't yet found a release for your dark moods and often lingering depression over your handicap, your health in later years may suffer - even worse than your short game.

Let the game's warmth and lighter moments sink into your body and soul. Golf is the elixir of youth! Maybe it can't make you younger, but lose the blues, let in the laughter, and golf can sure keep you from growing old!

Your Personal Fairways to the Glory of Golf

* *Don't be so fixed on studying all 837 divots you just pawed out of the practice range that you never look up to see all the birdies flying by.*

* *You truly live and die by your golf score. In many ways you have become your handicap, and wear it across your chest like a mug shot. Forget the numbers and you'll play better than ever.*

* *Chasing after lower golf scores is like trying to grab a handful of water. The tighter you squeeze, the less water you have – and the higher your handicap goes!*

* *Have the courage to let the child in you come out to play. Be a kid again. Ask yourself: "Are we having fun yet?" No? Then maybe it's time to tee it up on the miniature golf course. And leave your personal putting wand at home. Pick up a game with some real kids and get crazy!*

CAPRICORN

Capricorn Uncensored

"My swing is no uglier than Arnold Palmer's.
And it's the same ugly swing every time."
NANCY LOPEZ

"This is the hardest game in the world...
There is no way a golfer can think he is really something,
because that's when the game gets you."
BEN CRENSHAW

"I don't try to analyze my swing.
I looked at it once on film and almost got sick."
HUBERT GREEN

"Great champions learn from past experiences, whether those
experiences be good or bad. A lot of times a guy needs to be
knocked down before he gets up and fights."
PAUL AZINGER

"Look like a woman, but play like a man."
JAN STEPHENSON

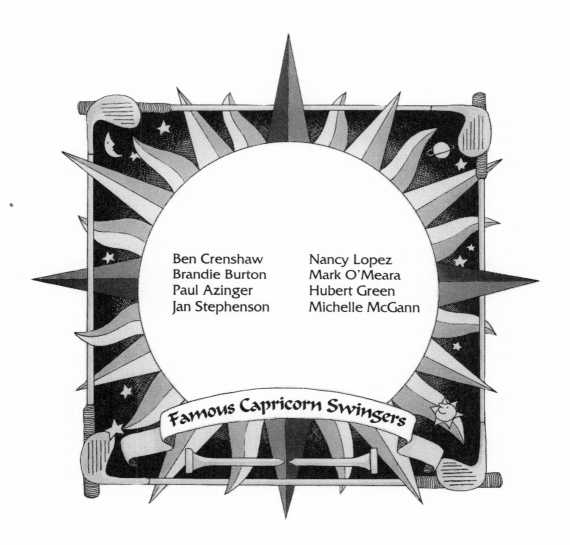

Ben Crenshaw   Nancy Lopez
Brandie Burton   Mark O'Meara
Paul Azinger   Hubert Green
Jan Stephenson   Michelle McGann

Famous Capricorn Swingers

CAPRICORN

AQUARIUS

January 20 – February 18

GOLFER

Your Celestial Golf Symbol

WATER BEARER

*You carry the heavy load of what you want the game to be -
not only for yourself, but for the rest of the world's golf enthusiasts.*

Your Golf Element

AIR

*The sky's the limit when it comes to realizing your golfing dreams.
Yours is a sign of friendship with the golfers of the world -
both to give and receive. Just ask fellow Aquarians, Jack Nicklaus,
Greg Norman and Micky Wright!*

Your Planetary Golf Guru

URANUS

*The sign of invention, independence and change.
You are not afraid to play golf in your own unique fashion,
inventing shots to fit every imaginable situation you get yourself into.*

Identifying the Aquarius Golfer

You are truly a breed apart. You know how impossible golf can be. You've experienced the worst it can give. You've been tortured and ridiculed in your quest to best old man par.

You know the game intuitively and have looked at all its blemishes from tee to green. You know only too well the agony and the ecstasy that awaits every time you tee it up.

And you wouldn't have it any other way. Because, like the game you love, you too can be unpredictable and shocking - particularly to those who don't understand the "bigger game" that you need to play.

You enjoy the never-ending challenge golf presents. Man against man, man against nature, man against himself - it's all there on the golf course and you are spellbound by it. No wonder you look like you're way out in "the zone" when playing your best.

There's more to you as a golfer than your handicap. It's how you go about the game that sets you apart from other players. You refuse to be classified under one label in terms of your golfing prowess - which can be awesome.

The guardian of golf's goodness, you believe in the eternal, universal quality of the game. If that makes you sound too good to be true, you'll fix that with some outrageous behavior that is anything but too good - yet true to your Aquarian nature.

"Some players weren't meant to win the U.S. Open.
Quite often, a lot of them know it."
JACK NICKLAUS

AQUARIUS

Portrait of the Female Aquarius Golfer

It is entirely possible for the Aquarius woman to have a meaningful relationship with golf, as long as she feels free to pursue other interests with other sets of friends.

Golf may be her game, but it's not the whole game, by any shot. There are so many other games to play, fairways to conquer, dreams to dream! She'll play by her set of rules and never let golf take so much of her time that she loses her freedom to try new things and meet new people.

The Aquarius female will never give so much of herself to golf that she neglects her need for diversity, intellectual interaction, revolt and occasional bizarre behavior.

Any real commitment to golf will generally find her involved in the betterment of the game for all womankind as an organizer, reformer or spokesperson.

If you're an Aquarius woman, you are not afraid to light up the course and let the wild shots fall where they may!

Portrait of the Male Aquarius Golfer

The Aquarian man can be completely hooked on golf - but until that happens, he's just testing.

He loves the people who do golf. The variety of golfers he encounters during a round fascinates and intrigues him.

The mystery of golf holds him hostage. The more he unravels its secrets and history, the more there is to know. Golf's eternal questions drive him to play his way toward discovery of all the answers. The more impossible, unfair and contradictory golf becomes, the more he is intoxicated by the challenge.

But if he ever finds the answers he's looking for, or the game doesn't live up to his high ideals, he'll toss the bag and sticks, and find a game that is worthy of his investigation.

How Aquarius Plays the Mind Game

You are ruled by your head rather than your heart and respond to mental stimuli. The courses and conditions of play that offer the most variety and challenge play right into your strengths.

The "Truth Seeker" of golf, you want to know where the game fits in the cosmic scheme of things. You can be detached, aloof, and possibly eccentric, but you have great ideas. You aren't afraid to tell them to the world and then do something about them.

How Aquarius Plays the Physical Game

While the physical part of golf is not your natural strength, you can rise to the top with a serious physical training program.

Once you get your footwork down and feel a good connection to the ground, you can improve your balance and tempo with practice. Any clumsiness or awkwardness that came as standard equipment with your Sun Sign can be overcome and even transformed into a major strength to compliment your mind game.

Best Part of the Aquarius Game

Your truthfulness about your abilities and your patience with the blossoming of those attributes gives you great advantage over your fellow players.

You are slow to anger and can put up with the worst the game can dish out for longer than the rest of us - which is worth at least a couple of shots per round.

Your creative powers to invent whatever shot is necessary lets you play better on the toughest courses where your mind is fully engaged for the entire round.

Traps'n Hazards

You are so interested in the larger game of golf that you don't pay enough attention to the game's normal, practical aspects. Little things like making sure you've got a glove, some tees, and a golf ball in your bag before it's your turn to tee off on the first hole.

The easier layouts, where everyone expects you to perform even greater feats of golfing glory, tend to bore you. And you don't hide it well.

Because Uranus relates to the electrical forces which flow through the nerve channels, your putting can be shaky at times. Now and again, you are prone to the "Yips."

Perfect Foursome

You appreciate the variety and mental stimulation Gemini brings to the game. Sagittarius provides the excitement you can never get enough of. And you can always use the extra helping of balance Libra delivers coming down the back nine.

Ideal Golf Courses

The world's toughest courses, of course! For openers take a hike to **Spyglass Hill** at Pebble Beach, California. Holes with names like Long John Silver and Black Dog don't intimidate you. And Spyglass' next door neighbor, **Cypress Point,** is as blissfully perfect as golf can get for Aquarius.

Here are a few more magnificent venues worthy of Aquarius' attention:

* **Pine Valley,** Pine Valley, New Jersey
* **Augusta National,** Augusta, Georgia
* **Pebble Beach Golf Links,** Pebble Beach, California
* **Merion, East,** Ardmore, Pennsylvania
* **The Country Club,** Brookline, Massachusetts
* **Winged Foot,** *West,* Mamaroneck, New York
* **Oak Hill,** *East Course,* Rochester, New York
* **Baltusrol,** *Lower Course,* Springfield, New Jersey
* **Oakmont,** Oakmont, Pennsylvania
* **Shinnecock Hills,** Southhampton, New York
* **Medinah,** *#3,* Medinah, Illinois
* **Muirfield Village,** Dublin, Ohio
* **The Olympic Club,** *Lake Course,* San Francisco, California
* **Royal Melbourne,** Australia
* **St. Andrews,** *Old Course,* Scotland

Best Colors to Wear While Playing

Since your Aquarius colors are electric blue, violet and indigo, go for a blue wardrobe when you need to transcend your earthbound handicap and raise your golfing to a higher plane.

Blue is very healing and can relax your nervous system. Your putting stroke can always use some of that!

Shooting Stars for Shooting Pars

* *Your nerves can betray all the assets you bring to the game. Stretch your feet and legs to loosen the tension, and your touch around the greens will be there when you need it.*

* *You can easily become diffused and absent-minded when it comes to golf's details. Get the necessary things in order before you tee off.*

* *Play less from your mind and more from the core of your being.*

The Aquarius Senior Swinger

You're always finding something new and exciting about golf for yourself and the world. But now's the time to tilt the balance toward you. There's only so much you can do for the world of golf.

Now, perhaps you can finally find that much needed equilibrium between your sense of duty to the world of golf and your sense of duty to the foursome and family closest to you.

Your Personal Fairways to the Glory of Golf

* *Knowing when to get your head out of the clouds will help bring your handicap back to Earth.*

* *Time to broaden your vision of the truths about your goals and needs as a golfer.*

* *Because your vision of golf is unique, you need to soften the impact of how you do things which can seem overwhelming to those who don't have your vision.*

* *Be true to yourself and your quest for the bigger truth will follow, as surely as Cypress Point will always be the "Sistine Chapel of Golf."*

* *You know the answers are not all in the technical aspects of the game. Tap into the buried treasure of emotion salted away deep inside and you will perform even greater feats of glory.*

AQUARIUS

Aquarius Uncensored

"Play each shot as if it's the first shot you're ever going to play.
The tournament starts on the next shot you hit."
GREG NORMAN

"When I play my best golf, I feel as if I'm in a fog...standing
back watching the Earth in orbit with a golf club in your hands."
MICKEY WRIGHT

"The truth is, my game was so good I sometimes felt,
well, almost bored playing golf."
BYRON NELSON

"I would rather play Hamlet with no rehearsal
than play golf on television."
JACK LEMMON

"No matter how hard I try, I just can't seem to break sixty-four."
JACK NICKLAUS

Micky Wright
Cary Middlecoff
Jim Thorpe
Judy Rankin

Patty Berg
Byron Nelson
Donna Caponi
Curtis Strange

Greg Norman
Jane Geddes
Sandy Lyle
Jose Maria Olazabol

Nick Price
Carol Mann
Marlene Hagge
Payne Stewart

Jack Lemmon
Jack Burke
Jack Benny
Jack Nicklaus

Famous Aquarius Swingers

AQUARIUS

PISCES

February 19 – March 20

GOLFER

Your Celestial Golf Symbol
FISH

You are lured by the deep, dark revelations about your hidden self that golf fishes
out of you, yanks to the surface and plays with until you
lie exhausted at the 19th hole shore.
Fortunately for Pisces, golf tends to be a "catch and release" sport.

Your Golf Element
WATER

Water signs deal with the subconscious,
so you can be secretive about your feelings for golf.
Your friends only see the calm surface of your golf waterline,
but have no idea of the strong current moving in deeper waters.
It's no surprise you enjoy courses where lakes or oceans come into play.

Your Planetary Golf Guru
NEPTUNE

Ruler of water hazards great and small, your on-course guru,
Neptune, inspires your intuition and imagination.
A dreamer, you need to balance your illusions of teeing off at famous pro/ams with
your intuition of what's "playable" in the practical world.

Identifying the Pisces Golfer

You are sensitive, emotional and truly concerned that others get as much out of golf as you do. The Pisces player is creative, artistic and often just as interested in painting the course or shooting pictures of it as shooting pars on it.

The fact that it's never easy to be the first salmon to reach the top of the stream is the very thing that attracts Pisces to golf's hidden meaning. Powerful currents play themselves out on every shot. Every fairway can reveal more than Pisces ever wanted to know about his or her true nature.

You may have an extensive golf library including such titles as: *Art & Zen of Learning Golf, Search For The Perfect Swing,* and *The Mystery of Golf.* While others may quote passages from Shakespeare, you quote pages from *Golf In The Kingdom,* and actually understand the last 75 pages!

Your instinctive tendency is to play golf with a lonely understanding too deep to share. Open up. Let it out, even if it's with the bartender at the 19th hole - who is probably a Pisces and will understand.

"I have never felt so lonely as on a golf course in the midst of a championship with thousands of people around."
BOBBY JONES

PISCES

Portrait of the Female Pisces Golfer

Golf loves you and welcomes you into its sorority with a hug and a kiss!

On the other hand, you may have to beat male golfers away with your 5-iron. In this age of hard driving women, your flowing femininity can be more attractive on the course than any actual shotmaking you do.

Golf doesn't treat the Pisces woman the way it does every other sign. While most of us are seduced by the game's mysteries, in your case, golf succumbs to your charms.

Or maybe it's just that you refuse to see how cruel and heartless the game can be. So what if you hit the ball 90 times or 129 times? You don't blame golf for all the awful things that happen to your ball. It's just the nature of the game.

The Pisces woman understands better than anyone what golf is all about. She doesn't have to be good to enjoy the golf trip. She just has to be on the ride.

Portrait of the Male Pisces Golfer

You often don't realize how good your game really is. You don't get crazy when you're off your stick and the putts aren't dropping, but you also don't always drink in the bubbles when your cup runneth over with pars and birdies!

When the Pisces can get his clever mind in tempo with his intuition and set a realistic goal for his golf performance, the results can be fame and fortune.

Because you are a romantic, the high-tech state-of-the-art world of metal golf technology is not your cup of titanium. For you there's nothing like the look and feel of woods actually made from wood!

How Pisces Plays the Mind Game

Not many people can see the game for what it is – the good, the bad, and the ugly – and then determine to accentuate the positive, eliminate the negative and laugh at the traps and hazards in-between.

You can be so forgiving of others, the course, the wind, and even the water hazards (usually your best friends), that you are more than happy to sail into today's round full of enthusiasm and hope.

The golf course is your canvas on which to create colorful scenes, and bold strokes of improvisation.

Isn't that what golf's all about?

It is for the passionate Pisces player.

How Pisces Plays the Physical Game

You could be the Baryshnikov of golf!

Whether tall and slender, or short and round, you are agile and light on your feet. Your hands are also a great asset, and when your swing is really in a groove, you hit the ball with little effort.

But because you use your body so much in communication, you can overdo. When you get too enthused, you can over-swing and lose control of your naturally good balance and tempo.

Because your body reflects so much of your Piscean soul for golf, you play better when you find a song to sing or hum as you glide down the fairway.

Best Part of the Pisces Game

Your imagination allows you to see all kinds of ways to play the most difficult shots. Trust it. Use it. Have more faith in your own unique talents. Any hacker can remember the past. You have the unique talent to "remember the future!"

Fellow Pisces swinger, Albert Einstein, said it best: "Your imagination is your preview of golf's coming attractions."

Traps'n Hazards

You become too easily disillusioned by your performance on the course, and then you withdraw and are afraid to play the game as only you can.

Get your head out of the stars. When you address the down-to-earth nature of golf - as it is and not as you wish it would be - you can do more for yourself and others who need your imagination and inspiration.

Perfect Foursome

Scorpio shares your passion and imagination. Deep inside you know you can learn a lot about course management from Virgo. You like the cool gamesmanship of Cancer - and their money to back up their game.

Ideal Golf Courses

Your artistic nature should find ample expression at *Torrequebrada Golf Club* in Spain where the course designer Pepe Gancedo is known as "The Picasso of golf course architecture."

You'll get a chance to play your old "sticks" at *Oakhurst* in White Sulphur Springs, West Virginia where the 9-hole course allows players to use only hickory-shafted clubs and replicas of gutta-percha balls.

Your imagination may hit overload when you play *Aberdeen* in Boynton Beach, Florida. Desmond Muirhead's design has holes shaped like a rattlesnake, a mermaid, the Loch Ness Monster, the Florida Keys, and Dolly Parton. There's also tributes to the Beatles, Henry Moore and Freud. Have fun!

But above all water is your natural playing partner and holds no fear for you. You would enjoy shooting pars and pictures at *River Islands* in Knoxville, Tennessee, an old logging site where five holes are on three islands in the French Broad River.

And *Caledonia Golf and Fish Club* in Myrtle Beach, South Carolina, was made for you. On Thursdays, the "catch of the day" is served after golf!

You have no trouble getting into the swim of things at the following courses:

* *Blue Monster* at Doral, Florida

* *Harbour Town,* Hilton Head Island, South Carolina

* *Grand Cypress,* Orlando, Florida

* *PGA National,* Palm Beach Gardens, Florida

* *Kemper Lakes,* Chicago, Illinois

* *Coeur d'Alene Golf Club,* Idaho

* *The Belfry,* Sutton Coldfield, England

* *Augusta National,* Georgia

PISCES

Best Colors to Wear While Playing

Wear the amorphous hues of chartreuse, olive and the quiet yellows, as well as contrasting colors like reddish orange and black. Almost anything with black resonates with the energy bubbling up from your deeper self.

Shooting Stars for Shooting Pars

* *Don't be so open to imaginative thinking that you confuse wisdom from golf gurus with wisecracks from golf goof-balls. (Though some times it's hard to tell the difference.)*

* *Strive for equilibrium between the romance of golf and the reality. Choose equipment that stresses function over good looks.*

* *The score you settle for on the card may be less important than the score you have to settle with yourself.*

The Pisces Senior Swinger

You still follow your heart, but now you begin to have a clearer view of the game of golf. Open others to your romantic vision; get them out of their limited view of golf "by the numbers." Share the excitement of colorful, creative strokes on the golf course canvas.

The Pisces senior golfer is like Old Man River. You just keep swinging along.

Your Personal Fairways to the Glory of Golf

*   *When your golf gets ugly, let off some steam instead of suffering in silence. You don't want to explode and wipe out yourself and the rest of your foursome.*

*   *Stop focusing on past performance. When you stop watering yesterday's divots, you will discover far more fairways in your future - and less unfair ones.*

*   *Play alone. It does your body and soul - and handicap - good. You need that quiet time on the course to nourish all your many golfing selves swimming in the dark water hazard of your soul.*

*   *For you, beating balls at the range can be a chore. Do it anyway. The more comfortable you become with your swing mechanics, the less you'll have to think about it on the course. Then you can fully use the creative instincts that serve your golf game so well.*

*   *Follow your heart. Don't let what others say keep you from playing and enjoying your magnificent obsession as only you know how.*

PISCES

Pisces
Uncensored

"Golf is a game of considerable passion,
either of the explosive type,
or that which burns inwardly and sears the soul."
BOBBY JONES

"You can buy a country, but you can't buy a golf swing.
It's not on the shelf."
GENE SARAZEN

"The pleasure derived from hitting the ball dead center
on the club is comparable only to one or two other pleasures
that come to mind at the moment."
DINAH SHORE

"If a bunch of duffers were around the bar thirty years from
now, I'd like to think they would remember me as a guy who
never forgot that golf is a game.
That when I shot 64, I wasn't a great guy
because I played well, and when I shot 87,
I wasn't a bad buy because I played poorly...."
PETER JACOBSON

"Have a blast while you last."
HOLLIS STACY

Bobby Jones
Sandra Palmer
Alice Ritzman
Peter Jacobsen

Tom Lehman
Dave Barr
Judy Dickinson
Jesper Parnevik

Amy Alcott
Andy North
Dinah Shore
Ian Woosnam

Gene Sarazen
Vijay Singh
Jeff Maggert
Hollis Stacy

Famous Pisces Swingers

PISCES

IS THAT ALL THERE IS?

Not by a long shot — or even a pitch and putt. There is a lot more to your birth connection to golf than the dominant traits associated purely with your Sun Sign — just as there's a lot more to you as a golfer than your handicap index number.

At best the information offered has confirmed and illuminated aspects of yourself that play an important part in how well you golf, giving you an even better shot at achieving your own personal best when you play.

At worst you won't have recognized anything about yourself, but noticed some traits of a few golfing friends. Except now you know how to play away from their strengths and how to exploit their weaknesses!

If that's where you're at, then don't share this book with any golfers you want to beat!

ABOUT THE AUTHOR

As founder of Golfaholics Anonymous® in 1984, Mark Oman believes that, "More is better. The more you enjoy playing, the better you become." To that end, Mark has written and sold over 300,000 copies of such humorous books as *PORTRAIT OF A GOLFAHOLIC, THE SENSUOUS GOLFER, WORLDS GREATEST GOLF EXCUSES* and *THE 9 COMMANDMENTS OF GOLF.*

During the last few years of his own awakening to various forms of personal enlightenment, Mark became intrigued by the concept of connecting our dominant Sun Sign personality tendencies to how we play the game of golf. For a Scorpio swinger like Mark, it should be no surprise that his passion to reach the unreachable pars is about to take us all on a trip to the stars!

Life must be lived as play.
PLATO, Greek Philosopher

Golf must be played to live!
OMAN, Fore-Play Philosopher

WILL A TRIP TO THE STARS REALLY BRING YOU PARS?

An Invitation to Play...

Anybody who's played this game for more than a week-and-a-half knows the truth. You can't hide from who you really are on the golf course. It all comes out – either willingly, or golf will drag it out of you kicking and screaming!

So, if we can't help but become our most true and genuine selves when we play, will making the most of our natural instincts and personality tendencies make us happier and better golfers?

You tell us. It's not enough that it works for me. We want to know from you! We'd love to hear what "teeing it up" with *GOLF ASTROLOGY* as a playing partner does for you.

We look forward to hearing the stories of your personal journey down these "fairways less travelled" to the glory of the game.

You are invited to write us, FAX, or just holler, "Fore!"

Your golf experiences – the good, the bad, the beautiful, or the outrageous – may end up in a future book. We will credit you by name or protect your anonymity as you wish.

Or just write to "play around."
Golf Astrology
c/o Golfaholics Anonymous®
P.O. Box 222357, Carmel, CA 93922
(408) 624-4386 or FAX (408) 626-9357

OTHER BOOKS BY MARK OMAN

**THE SENSUOUS GOLFER –How To Play The Game...
On The Course And Off!**
Illustrated by Tom Nix
(72 pages – 32 illustrations)
ISBN#0-917346-01-7

Whether you keep it in your bag or under your bed, this book will put you in a position to play around with the best of 'em!

**WORLD'S GREATEST GOLF EXCUSES –All the GOOD Reasons for
Playing so BAD in the 1990's**
Illustrated by Doug Goodwin
(112 pages – 36 illustrations)
ISBN#0-917346-03-3

In the 1990's you're going to need a whole bagful of inspired, high-tech excuses. Because when you're playing your WORST – only the BEST excuses will save the day!

**THE 9 COMMANDMENTS OF GOLF...According to The Pro
Upstairs–Cosmic Secrets for Mastering the Game!**
Illustrated by Doug Goodwin
(112 pages – 20 illustrations)
ISBN#0-917346-07-6

Dial direct to your higher self...Put trust in your gut...And behold the Glory of Golf, as it is in Heaven and ought to be on Earth!